MORE TRUTH

Communicated by

ARTHUR FINDLAY

His initial experience of
life after death, given
through the mediumship of
Eileen Winkworth

Harmony
PRESS LTD

I come to bring a sequel to my work
that I did upon the earth plane.
I wish for what is come to be called,
simply,

MORE TRUTH

ARTHUR FINDLAY

Acknowledgements
To my friends of both worlds,
without whose love and support
this work would not have been
brought forward.

E.W.

First published in Great Britain 1985
by Harmony Press Ltd. Reading

ISBN 0 946899 01 0

Set in Bembo by JH Graphics Ltd., Reading

Made and printed in Great Britain by Cox and Wyman Ltd., Reading

Introduction

Arthur Findlay, who died in 1964, devoted over 40 years of his life to the task of proving the existence of life after physical death.

His work began after this initially sceptical Scottish lawyer received overwhelming evidence from direct voice medium John C. Sloan one memorable September night in 1918. He was so impressed that he went home and wrote till the small hours of the next morning, a careful account of all that had occured. This was the beginning of a long and careful investigation into Spiritualism, and Arthur Findlay wrote many books during his lifetime. His first, and perhaps best known, is a wonderful introduction to Spiritualism for the enquirer. On the Edge of the Etheric – survival after death scientifically explained – was first published in 1931 and ran to more than 60 editions, with translations made in nineteen different languages.

During the years of his investigation Arthur Findlay moved to England. In 1923 he bought Stansted Hall, a magnificent house and estate at Stansted Mountfitchet in Essex, where he came to live with his family in 1928.

Stansted Hall was left to the Spiritualists National Union by Arthur Findlay when he passed in 1964, and now it houses the Arthur Findlay College. This is administered by the SNU as a residential centre where students can study Spiritualist philosophy and religious practice, spiritual healing, spiritual and psychic unfoldment, and other kindred disciplines.

Janet A. Leggott

Contents

CHAPTER 1

My Transition into Spirit Life

'I J. Arthur Findlay, being of sound mind . . . ' This seems a very final statement when you sit with your solicitor and draw up your last Will and Testament to be placed in a safe place of keeping until you have passed into spirit life. And yet, when I stood and listened to the Will being read after I had passed into spirit, I thought – how wonderful to be free of earthly burdens and material considerations. How lucky I was, at last, to be able to go into the spiritual realms to find out for myself what is true and what is not true of what others have said to me whilst I was on the earth plane. And I was pleased to leave that room and to go forward into the light, the golden light that was shining ahead of me with the ones who were waiting, and beckoning me to come forward.

There were many friends who were gathered, too numerous to mention, but there was my old friend, Sloan, who was there to greet me. He placed his hand upon my shoulder and said, 'Come, let us go forward together to find more spiritual truth and understanding', and, as we walked along the road, it was like walking into another dimension. We were filled with happiness and lack of care. I felt so light in heart, something I had not done for years because of the burdens of responsibility that had been upon me. I knew that now I would be able to go forward and to probe and to ask others who had made the transition how it came about that they were there and what they had done in their lives to bring them into this lovely place that I now find myself in.

I saw the crystal streams, things that had been explained to me be other people in other books I had read – books that people ridiculed because it had seemed as though it was a fairy story that was being told – and yet, here was I, able to put my hand into the crystal streams. Able to feel the coolness of the water, and yet, to withdraw my hand and find it still dry; to be able to taste the fruit of the trees as I pass along my way; and to be able to see the flowers and to smell their perfumes, more enhanced than ever they were when I was on the earth plane.

I, myself, found it difficult to contain my soul within myself where I felt so elated. The mind that went with me is still clear and able to calculate and accumulate the beauty that was around me. We know that there are places that are not so beautiful for those who have not yet seen light but I, somehow, have been fortunate, and the light is here around me and I am thankful to my Maker for this light.

Many people think that when they pass into spirit they will see religious figures of great standing – the Christed ones – but no, there is no need, because their light helps to shine, bringing more light to the area in which I am travelling.

I am pleasantly surprised by seeing friends and the understanding that is quickly between us because there are no words. There is no need for words. The thoughts are there and so each understands one another's thoughts. There is a beautiful build-up of love that is felt. It is not very easy to put it into words, or to make any understanding of it, but it is something within yourself that seems to be bursting out towards others with a joy of being able to be near someone whom you have known and spent time with upon the earth plane.

I am lucky because I know that I will be helped by my friends and I will find understanding from the ones who come from higher up who will be able to help me to achieve what I want to do.

I want to travel through the halls of learning to find true understanding of my fellow man. But first, I know that I must go to the place of judgement. The place I must go to see how my true pattern of life has worked out, where you are shown the blueprint that you were shown when you were coming first from spirit life into human life, and then the result of when you return. The one blueprint is placed over the other, so that you can see the deviations you have made. Then comes the mental remembrance of all the things that you have done – the thoughtless word, the unkind act – these are more important than anything else. It is what you have thought within yourself, and the actions you have made, that makes the difference between right and wrong.

Man's concept of God, and of sin, and of human conduct is totally different from that here on the spirit side of life and what is judged. You judge yourself, my children. You look at your life and you see, clairvoyantly, you would say, pictures of your life, and this, in itself, can be a punishment when you know that you hurt someone's feelings.

Then you go on from that place to find the abode which you, in your life, have built up for yourself. The true meaning of what your life has been. The environment that you have lived in, and have not felt comfortable in, is not there, but there is something beautiful in the area in which you are now able to live. You will find comfort in the coolness of the breeze, in the scent and perfumes from the garden, in the shade from the summer sun which you have when you enter into the house; and the beautiful perfume that pervades into the housing area. There are no doors or walls. It seems as though it is eternally Spring here.

You are warm, and not cold in any way. You feel the movement of air around you and the movement of everything. It seems as though everything is a shimmering myriad of light much as you would see in the desert – a mirage that shimmers in the light – and this is how it is in the spirit world because it is built of such fine vibrations. Like gossamer threads built together to make a twine, and it is exceedingly beautiful to see and to experience. Music is around you, in the very air that you breathe, in the very essence of the flowers, in the very light that is about you. You hear this music as though it is coming on the wind. We know, on the earth plane, people put chimes by their doors so that the wind can take them and make them move to play beautiful music, but here there are no chimes and yet the music is most wonderful.

You do, from time to time, hear the heavenly choirs, but these come, funnily enough, from orthodox-looking churches that are placed along the way. Many people still stick religiously to their beliefs and they do not wish to let them go and, as we pass, we feel sorry for them because we know it will be quite some time before enlightenment will come to them so they will see that there is no need for buildings. It is what is truly inside of you, your thoughts towards God and his presence with you that count.

There are many things that I could say. I know that it may seem as though I repeat myself when I speak of the beautiful light, but when you see all the colours of the rainbow shimmering around you it is like you are caught in a prism of light and it is beautiful. You seem to radiate health all over. What took you into spirit does not matter anymore, it is not with you. You are made whole and you are happy and content.

As you go on your way you see children playing and you see happiness in their faces and you hear laughter in your ears. You know that these children, when they left the earth plane, must have left much sadness behind them for their parents and yet, here they are, quite content and happy, being taken care of by others who love children, who will give them the understanding and help they need on our side of life.

As I go on I see the beautiful water that is there. It is just as though you are walking on a seashore. It seems as though your mind only has to think of these things and they are there. It is as though the mind controls everything and you are able to conjure up these pictures in your mind and yet, if you put your hand in the water, you know that there is a vital force and it is a living thing. You see the grandeur of the forests and the trees. It seems as though you only have to think it and they are there with you.

I, myself, think of my home in my own country and I see all things. I see the rolling hills and the vales, the 'glens' as they were called then, but I say 'vales' now because I spent much time in England and I have grown used to using their language also beside my own. I see the heather on the hills and I hear the grouse as they fly across the moor, and I am pleased again because my heart is flying with them. But I do not hear the shooting going on that I used to hear. When I was a boy, I used to cringe when I thought of these beautiful birds being shot and killed just to grace someone's table. Do not mistake me, I have eaten them myself, but I still think of them and of the beauty of their flight which I see now before me in this kaleidoscope of life.

Again I am walking. The peace that is with me is wonderful. It seems as though I have left the others behind me in my eagerness to go forward and to search and to find, and yet, I only have to think of my companions and again they are with me.

It is a wonderful thing, this power of thought. Man does not realise what he has – what potential – when he is on the earth plane. He little realises how much is wasted effort and how much could be done with the power of thought being directed in the right way to help his fellow man.

As I am walking now and thinking, I am thinking of the loved ones who I have missed. But Sloan reads my thoughts and places his hand upon my shoulder and says to me, with mind thought, 'Be patient, for, in a little while, all things will adjust. Then you will be able to see them, and you will find understanding as to why they were not there to meet you because of the jobs and other things that they are doing to help mankind'.

There are many people who draw close now. It seems as though there is a meeting of some sort going on and there seems to be someone who is speaking to the others. I am sending out thought now towards this person so that I listen and I hear someone speaking of the 'truths' and 'understandings' of life. It seems that he, when he was on the earth plane was an orator and wishes still to make himself heard and that other people should listen to his views. But Sloan sends thought out to me, and says, 'Feel sorry for him because he still has self to overcome, but it will come in time. He is a goodly soul, this is only one fault. You must not look for faults in others, but you must look into yourself and think, 'I am glad that that fault is not with me today'.

Time seems to hang like a thread. It seems as though, although I have walked a long way, that I am neither tired, nor have I noticed the passage of time. It has gone on and I am quick to understand the full meaning that time is endless. There is no end or beginning to it, and it is like being in suspended animation here. As though you are being cocooned in warmth and light away from care so that you are able to put your mind at ease and be at peace with your soul.

I think for ones who first come into spirit life that many of us have thoughts of our old lives that we bring with us. We worry about those left behind, and yet, we know that there is no need for worry because help is being given from both sides – from the spirit world and from the material world – towards those people, helping them to find love and understanding.

I am beginning to understand the full meaning of 'mediums' now. I was, at one time, very doubtful, until Sloan became my companion, and then I found understanding. I knew that he was a person of integrity and that he would not let me down. Now I realise that there is much work for mediums upon the earth plane to bring hope to people who are bereaved, who have lost loved ones, and can find no solace. I know that there are many times when mediums are decried because they do not always seem to come up to standard, but who are we to judge? Whether or not they can ever fit into a specific standard of work will be according to the mental capacity of the medium being used. Do they have potential enough to be used by higher souls, or will they stay on the same level, and give their work according to that level of intelligence that comes through them.

Many people do not realise that, with mediumship, there are many things that can cause, as you would say, the record not to play straight. It is like when you play the phonograph and you find the needle sticks. This is a thing that cannot be helped because sometimes there is a fault in the machine that causes it to stick on that particular place and marks the record. This causes a groove to be formed that should not be there, and I think that sometimes, in a medium's mind, this happens with **bad training. The needle sticks in the groove and it cannot be** released, so higher souls cannot come through that medium because of the damage that has been done by bad training. I think, myself, that there are a lot of faults that are put down to the medium's personality that have nothing to do with personality but to do with the training of that medium in the first place.

I think that education is not necessary, because, in my own lifetime, I have heard mediums who have had no education being used by quite brilliant intellects that have come from the spirit world to use them. I, myself, am going to look into this very deeply from this side of life to see if I can find out how the 'mechanics' of mediumship really work. I was taught very much when I was on the earth plane from the 'seances' that I attended with Sloan. I was able to find the knowledge, to get answers and to be helped, but I still feel that there is much that is left unsaid. This needs to be unravelled and looked into, and I feel that, now I am here, this is my job – to be able to do these things and to be able to bring forward to people the true meaning of 'a medium'.

As I went forward again, it felt as though night was coming and yet the light did not alter. I felt as though I needed to rest; but this was not the weariness I felt on earth; just a mental tiredness as though I wanted to close my eyes for just a little moment of time – and I would be all right again.

I feel Sloan's hand upon my shoulder. He reads my mind and beckons unto me, and so I find myself again within that shimmering mirage that I call a dwelling, and I see a lovely couch to lie on. I will lie and rest a while because I feel that it is important that I rest now so that I will be prepared for the journey that is farther ahead. I know that I will travel many roads in my quest to find more truth.

CHAPTER 2

My New Beginning

I have awakened and I feel refreshed, and the words come to mind, 'To sleep, perchance to dream'. I feel that all I have experienced has been but a dream, a myth in time, and now that I am refreshed, I shall go forward to more adventure and more thought in this new world that faces me. I look about me and I see the animals playing and the birds in the trees, the fruit, and the flowers. They are beautiful. I wish I could put pen to paper to describe to you the beauty of this world. It is so different and unspoiled. You do not see a leaf or a petal that is damaged. Somehow this fades away and only perfection is here. You see truth and understanding in the faces of the people who are around and about you.

At first you are not aware of people and then, suddenly, they seem to be there beside you as though they have just faded in to your line of thought. It is surprising how powerful thought is. Man does not realise his full potential when he is on the earth plane. He does not realise the true gift from God in the brain that we take so much for granted, in our own personalities, and in our own minds. The brain is just a vessel to be used and yet Man uses it wrongly. He does not fulfil everything that he could in his earth life.

Now I am in spirit life I look forward to again seeing my friends and my relatives and my dear wife. I know that she will be somewhere waiting for me to join her, but I must reach the full realisation of my passing and being in spirit first. I hear many names being called towards me as though I am listening to echoes from the past. They seem to come then fade away and I feel that I must train my mind to be able to accept these names as they come and to be able to place them. How many times have people listened to mediums when they have given messages from the platforms, saying, 'I have someone here of this name', and the person says, 'I'm sorry, I do not recognise that name, so I cannot accept'. I must listen now so that I can truly understand and realise who these people are who are interested in me in this new state of my life.

Many people say that, when you pass into spirit, you go through a tunnel or through a great light, and yet, for me, it seemed as though there were none of these things. It seemed as though I was fully aware immediately of the situation and I was able to grasp and to cope with my thoughts at that moment of time. I will admit that, at first, my mind was very full of thought – What happens now? What happens next? What happens to my property? What happens to the future of different things? Will my books be republished? Will anybody read my books now I am passed into spirit? Will anybody remember me? – and all these foolish things go through your head. But, at last, common sense prevails and you start to analyse the situation and to think, 'Well, I know that I am in spirit life now so I must gather my thoughts. I must think. "What must I do? What can I do? What will I do"'. Then, as you begin to see people drawing close into your range of thought, you realise that there is nothing you have to do. Whatever is necessary for you will be shown to you at the right time and in the right place.

Suddenly I felt as though I was tired. I did not realise that I was going to go into a sleep state, yet the first recollection I had was of waking, refreshed and renewed. So I understand now that, when it is necessary for me to rest it will come and overtake me as tiredness did with the old body but not quite in such a heavy way. It is just a little thought of tiredness, and then release from that tiredness comes. So it is with regard to food. I have looked about me and I have thought, 'Well, should I feed this heavenly body or will it be alright without food and drink'? Yet I have tasted the fruit of the tree and found it very palatable and it seemed to be refreshing. With regard to drink, the water here is sparkling, it is not unlike tonic water that we have on the earth plane and, as you drink it, it seems to bubble upon your tongue and yet you do not feel as though anything has gone down your throat, you understand. It feels as though it just tingles and bubbles in a delightful way and there is no need for you to swallow because there is nothing there to swallow. And so you realise that this is just an experience you are having and not an actual thing. It is something that your mind has thought of and thought you had need of, and then you realise that this is not so.

I think, in this new adventure, I will find there are many things that I will conjure up with my mind because I will think that I will need them and then find that, after all, it was not necessary. I feel sure that, as I journey on, I shall be shown many things and many truths will be proven to me that I could not have accepted when I was on the earth. Things my friends have talked about, when I have listened to them and said, 'Well, I cannot quite accept that, so I will store it in my mind to see if later on I can put it into its own pigeon-hole'. I know now, that, with this new life, there will be many things that will be pigeon-holed and many things that I will have to re-think and understand. I know my friends who have passed on into spirit before me will have patience and they will come and help me. I look forward to seeing my old friends. It seems as though Sloan has left me for a while because I cannot see him anywhere, and yet I know he is not far away because I feel his influence with me. I feel his thought pattern towards me and I feel this thought pattern is very important because it is a thing of this life and not of the old life.

It is strange that, although when I was on the earth plane I was a meticulous keeper of time, I have not missed my watch that I carried with me in my pocket. I have not missed looking at it because, somehow, now, it seems so unimportant that time should be counted. As I am now, I feel the gentle passage of this life, but it is not the 'hustle and bustle' that I was used to upon the earth plane. It was that sort of life that drew me away to live in country surroundings and, even now, in my mind's eye, I can see the park around me and I see the trees – the copper beeches – and I see my tulip tree. But, funnily enough, it is easy for the mind to conjure up these things here. As I have said to you, thought is the mother of invention, and to think means it is here with me, not just a memory, but something that I can see with my mind's eye.

But enough is said now of the beauties of this place for the time being because there is someone who is approaching me and beckoning me to go forward with him. He has a robe on which is a myriad of colours and yet is translucent, pink and grey. I feel quite content to walk at his side because I know that he will help me and guide me forward. He speaks in his mind to me as an old friend, telling me that he had often walked with me upon my earth journey and that he had been a constant companion to me through my childhood and adult life. Now I begin to see the true significance of his presence. For want of a better name, he must have been my 'spiritual guide' when I was in my earthly body. He talks to me in his mind. It is so easy, the thought transference between us is so simple and yet so meaningful. He shows me the path along which I must travel. He says that it is important for me to start at the very beginning and to go forward, so he is showing me now that there are other spheres of life here. Not just the comfortable ones that I have seen to approach, but ones that are not so comfortable. He is intent on showing me all things and all facets of this life.

I see magnificent buildings as I pass and enquire, with my mind, of him, could he please tell me what the buildings are and what they are used for. He nods and says that there are many halls of learning, but it is necessary for me to be shown other things first so that I will truly appreciate them when I am shown them later. As I am walking, it seems as though the way is less protected and more overgrown. It seems as though the gardeners of heaven have not been quite so efficient in this spot. It seems as though I am going forward and yet I feel the grass toughening under my feet as though it is of a coarser nature. The atmosphere seems to be altering.

It seems to be less light and airy, and I feel as though there is a mist that is arising around us that makes it not quite so clear to discern things. Things become as they are when you are in a fog, when you see only wisps of clarity and then fog again, but it is not so dense that I cannot see the surroundings and the people who are moving around. They do not seem to be quite as alert as I feel and they seem to shuffle along their way. It is as though they are so taken up with themselves that they do not see the people that are around them. They do not see the brightness of the robe of the one I am travelling with because they do not even put a glance towards him or myself.

It seems as though they only have eyes to see themselves and their immediate environment. I send out thought toward the one who is guiding me, saying please could he explain to me why it is so foggy here and there seems to be this denser attitude and altitude, (I feel a denser attitude of mind and less rarified altitude). He sends thought to me to say that these people have been so wrapped up in their material conditions before they left the earth plane that, at this moment of time, they cannot adjust and realise that conditions can be better than they faced upon the earth. He says this is sometimes the case of people who have had to work hard for their living and who have grasped, and hung on to, everything that they have made in case they needed it and shared nothing with others. These people are in this environment until they can see light pervading into the atmosphere, and then they will be able to go forward and to move into a higher plane of thought.

As I am walking now, it seems to be quite rocky in places and I am fearful that I may stumble but he puts his hand out. No word is spoken between us but the thought reaches him and he smiles at me and gives me his hand as if to say, 'I will help you along the way'.

As I go, I am becoming quite aware that there are people who have no light with them at all. It seems as though everything is darkening and everything is grey. I cannot see any colour at all in anything. There is no colour to the trees or the houses as we pass by. Everything has this drab, grey hue and everything seems to be the same as the next. Each building is the same as the other, none has any difference. It seems as though the same hand has built them and there is no change of character to any of the dwellings. I say 'dwellings' because they are little more than this. Whoever lives here must have a very poor existence of life and mind. Again, he smiles at me and sends thought to me to say, 'These people had no thought for others, only for their own selfishness, and so they cannot see beyond themselves. Feel sorry for them. Pray for them, that light may come into this part of their atmosphere'.

Now I am quite weary. I am feeling tired because of the weight of the feeling that is with me. I feel as though I have the weight of the world's problems upon my shoulders. As I walk, it seems to squelch underfoot as though it is marsh that I am walking on. I feel as though my legs no longer have any energy to put one foot in front of the other.

I begin to see that these places are not like dwellings at all, but are more like the cave dwellers must have had in ancient times. I see the marks of the walls where water has corroded the rock and there is a smell of mud and pestilence here. I feel it is a very unclean atmosphere.

People seem to be without shape or form – almost as if they had no body the same as I, as though they were just shapes and no substance – and they seem to be without movement and without power of thought transference because I am picking up no thoughts from these people at all. It is as though they are like dumb animals and cannot see with their eyes. I feel as though their eyes are blinded to this light and this world and that the scales must be lifted from their eyes before they will ever be able to see.

Yet, as I look, I see beams of light working around them closely, watching them and seeming to monitor their actions and their thoughts. It is as though they are being constantly watched in conditions, we would say, like laboratory animals; where they are noted for their habits and their problems and a document is filled out denoting which animal has which tendencies. I feel as though this existence, on this plane of thought, must be very limited and I would say that whoever lived here would not be in a pleasant state of mind. Yet these workers of light are there constantly. You see their light about them, shining out even in this dark gloom, but, as to whether or not the scales will be lifted from the eyes of these beings so that they will absorb some light, will be another thing. I think it will take many years for light to ever penetrate here in this atmosphere. I look at the one who stands beside me and he reads my thoughts. 'You and I must leave now because I am so weary that I feel I could not walk back.'

He smiles and takes my elbow and seems to usher me out into less gloom and gradually, as I walk, my feet become lighter and I am walking back now towards the plane of thought that is my area of living. As I walk, he is constantly sending thoughts towards me, helping me to understand fully that God does not turn his back on anyone, that everyone has a chance to see light. Even in the darkest gloom the bright light of the 'workers of light' is there so that anyone who sees may ask for help.

As I go on my step becomes much lighter and I feel as though I have more vigor. More feeling of 'goodness' is with me, as though a weight has been lifted off my mind, as though I have less to think of and not so many worries. I feel that those people who are there must feel as though they have the worries of the universe upon their heads.

He smiles at me again and takes me forward. I see that now I am passing through a beautiful garden. I see the colours of the birds in the trees and, as they come across the lawn, it seems not as though they hop but as if they glide. They seem comfortable, and able to merge with the atmosphere. I see a lovely lake that is formed there and the beauty of the stonework around it. Everything here seems to be perfect, more like I would imagine the Garden of Eden to be, that was written of many years ago in the orthodox Bible.

I look at my guide and he smiles and says to me by thought, 'Rest awhile, absorb the chlorophyll in the trees and the grass, absorb everything that is important to you, the colours, because this is healing upon your soul. You have dispelled and spent much energy in the small walk you had with me this day because you have seen how heavily life can weigh upon people and how people who have not spent their lives thinking of others will have much to think of when they come into the spiritual side of life.

I am now walking through an orange grove. I look, but I cannot quite comprehend the different ways that all flowers and fruit can grow together. Although in our own environment we find that different countries can produce different fruits because of climatic conditions, here everything grows in profusion. When I look at the small flowers and see the delicate petals, and smell the perfume, and examine the blooms, I see no imperfections. It seems as though anything not perfect cannot survive here. I feel this is how thought must be here. Perfect thought, thought of kindness towards others in need, thought towards those upon the earth plane who are still struggling in their earthly life. Then I start to think of my home and wonder how things are there; whether or not my wishes will be carried out to the letter or whether someone will adjust my wishes to suit themselves. But then he looks at me and smiles as if to say, 'Enough for today. Leave thoughts behind you now and absorb the light here. Rest awhile.' Suddenly I feel a little tiredness as I have done before and I know that it is time for me to sleep again to refresh my soul.

I will take you further with me on my next journey because I know there will be many journeys I must make in this life; many people I must meet and talk with before I shall ever be able to fully comprehend the true meaning of the universe that I have left behind and the power and love of our Father, God.

CHAPTER 3

My Pathway Through Light

Again, I seem to be as though I am moving forward. I feel very refreshed and happy. The one who walked by my side is here again and he takes my hand and leads me forward. Today I know that I will learn many truths and these truths will be proven to me beyond doubt. I look forward to finding light and understanding in this beautiful place. As movement takes me forward it seems as though I am not walking this time, as if I am propelled by thought alone, as if, by thought, I am being taken from one place to another. (I have heard that in the spirit world everything begins and ends with a thought and now I am beginning to understand this movement that there is with thought.) I am going forward and being shown a different area of life. It is as though I am looking back over my past existence. Perhaps this, to me, is what is normally called, 'the Day of Judgement.' Perhaps today I will really be able to see how my life has truly been lived. I find myself moving towards a beautiful building which shimmers white in the light here, yet it does not dazzle the eyes. It seems as though it is made translucent so one can accept it and not be worried by the brightness there. As I pass into the building I am aware that there is much coming and going. There seem to be many people who are walking in pairs, such as I and the one who is walking with me, as though they also are being taken there for a purpose.

Now I am entering a small room and there is a desk with a plan upon it. It is just like a blueprint that you see for buildings and yet it is not of the same textured paper or of the same patterning of thought. To me, as a layman, it looks like a family tree – as though someone has traced their history back and sees the branches of their family. Yes, it is a family tree! I can see, beyond doubt, that this belongs to me. There is a duplicate by the side of it and I feel as though I want to place one on top of the other to see how much different they are. I can see that there are intricate patterns upon this paper (yet it is not paper. It feels like parchment, yet it is clear). I see that, although there are similarities of pattern in places, there are great changes and spaces where perhaps no progress seems to have been made in the drawing of the structural filament. I know this is a very awkward way to describe it and yet I cannot describe it in other words. I feel as though there was a change in my life that did not fit into the pattern of the life I chose to come into. I feel as though I must have, in many places, deviated from my true path of life. As these thoughts come to me I look at my companion and he is smiling and nodding as if to say to me, 'Yes, you are now in full understanding that this is different from the way you chose it to be.'

I sit here with my eyes closed now and it feels as though my head is registering many pictures. Pictures from memory, taking me back to my early days on the earth plane – memory that I could not recall when I was still in my earthly existence because our memories seem to close down in certain areas of thought and we cannot recall our very early childhood. I see myself here being born, progressing through walking stage, through school and going onward and I begin to see that perhaps, in some ways, I was not quite such a good scholar as I should have been or perhaps quite such a good son as I should have been. As I am going forward I see different changes coming in, spiteful things that I inadvertantly did. I see myself pulling the wings off a fly now and I remember how clever I thought I was at that time. When I recall this memory now, it makes me think how cruel I was to imprison a fly so that it could not move and have its mobility in life. I know it may seem a trivial incident and yet it had purpose to teach me a lesson.

As I go forward I see myself in early manhood, on the threshold of life. I feel very ambitious and forward–looking, pushing and wanting to succeed, yet I know that there are others who would be hurt by my actions, especially my own parents who would think that I was not following in the family's footsteps. I see there were many thoughts that they had for me, and promise of future developments which I, with my foolish ideals, put away from them. As I go on I see much of my personal life and, although I thought I did my best, I see that I could have been a better person. I could have been more understanding and thoughtful in many ways. I followed my quest for spiritual knowledge and put this beyond many things, yet I do not feel that I did wrong because I know there are many people upon the earth plane who seek the truth and light and never, ever find it.

I am going forward now at a more rapid pace and I see many things in my personal life. These are personal to me, which I would not tell you because they are my own personal lessons in life that I had to learn, and I begin to realise, truly, God's wisdom and His love when He gave us freedom of will. He did not want us to be regimented like soldiers so that we were all the same. He wanted us to have our faults and our blessings, and in life these things are given to you. It is how you use the gifts you have that determines whether or not you will reap a just reward. Do not look, my friends, for reward upon the earth plane. Do not think that everything is yours by right. You have to earn the right for many things and, in doing so, you will find that your character alters and you become a better and wiser person. I see the callow youth I was when I first started out on my first steps of life. I see that, towards the end of my life, I did make some good decisions – decisions that would help others in the future to carry on with my thoughts. To move forward into a more 'open' way of thinking with regard to thoughts of God and the powers of the Universe and beyond.

Now my friend stands up, as if to say to me, 'This part is over. You have recognised things here that you have done and said and your thoughts have registered and there is nothing for you to worry about because this part of coming here is over. Now we shall go on to greater things.' As I come from this place, I feel light in heart, as though a burden has been lifted off my shoulders and I know now that I, in facing my life, have accepted the responsibility for my actions. So, you see, it is again the fifth principle – responsibility for your own actions upon the earth plane. There is much truth in the seven principles. We know that sometimes people do not like, or wish to hear, principles put forward. They like to formulate their own opinions. But today, my personal responsibility was shown to me and I accept it.

Now I am going forward and I feel overjoyed because I know that I am being taken into a great library. It is a beautiful place! It is light and airy and it seems as though the windows are of crystal because the light shines so bright through them, so clearly and precise. I see the rows of books and I am moved to touch the bindings. I am surprised not to feel them hard, as earthly books with leather bindings, but soft and pliable, yet durable and light. As I lift a book and take it from its place I see quite clearly that this book is not of earth but of here, and I realise that it is someone's synopsis to their life story. As though there was something that they had to put right so they set to with pen and paper and started an autobiography of their life cycle. I see that, in this case, this person has been very self-critical and very understanding of the faults that they had. It is a woman who has written this book and, as I read, I start to think as that female and I can understand how her mind must have been when she wrote this book. It is as though, by taking the book from the shelf, I am taking over her personality and her life and I feel completely absorbed in this. It is as though I am reliving it myself. It is a very unusual experience and I feel as though, although this person had much to learn when she came into spirit life, by writing the book there was much that was put right.

Now I seem to be moving away from that section of the library. I am drawn towards books that are copies of earth books and I see that there are many famous writers. My friend looks at me and the thought comes forward, 'You can read "before" spirit life and then "after" spirit life because you will find there is a vast difference in the thoughts of these people once they have passed into the spirit world and begin to find their perspective.' I am beginning to understand because I have been a writer of books myself. I know now that I have a task ahead because I must review my own books and then write my opinions on what has been written in earth life by me. This, in itself, will be a mammoth task and I look at him with a pleading in my heart that perhaps I will be given help and understanding in this task. His thought comes to me, 'You will be given what is right at the right time. There is no need for you to worry or hurry because time here is not measured as in earthly life and you will find the time to be able to cope. Time from ahead and time from behind and time from now is as one, so that we never run out of time here.'

I am going forward again and seeing many people. They are sat quietly or in groups and they seem to be discussing, but there is no noise because it is thought, so it disturbs no-one. As I pass by the table I pick up their thoughts on many things. I find that they are groups of people who have been in many religions. There is one group who are Catholic, another who are non-conformist, and they, in their way, are reviewing their thoughts on Christianity and on God. I see that there are quite a few who are really indoctrinated into their own form of religion and who have to spend many years or days here discussing and thinking before their minds will be open enough for full understanding and light to come forth to them. As I look at them, I think to myself, 'Oh, God, am I not lucky to have found light while I was still on the earth plane, that I had a glimmer of hope before I came and that I knew one day I would gain more understanding and knowledge. I do not say "full" understanding because I know that there is much involved before I will ever gain, as I would say, full understanding.'

As I go forward, I hear music and I am drawn along a beautiful corridor. There is a colonnade of marble posts along this place. I see busts upon these posts and I recognise faces of musicians who have passed into spirit life. It seems as though they are all depicted here and underneath the busts are the names. I see Debussy, Brahms and many others and I wonder why there have to be these effigies for people to look at. Then I realise that they are not really effigies, they are just in my own mind because I am hearing strains of their music. Thus, things form in my mind to bring forward these busts of the composers. I am very pleased with music I hear because it is such a sweet and gentle sound. I hear all kinds of instruments being used and yet it is gentle music. There is nothing strident here and I feel as though I am being wafted along on warm air. I feel as though everything is being bathed in the music and that the music comes with colour. It is most awe-inspiring. It is as if every note that is played leaves the instrument and changes into a droplet of colour and, as the music is being played, so these droplets are shimmering in the light. I feel as though, even if I were blind, I would be able to see this because it is so beautiful.

I see many young children who are practising and playing on pianos and instruments that seem too big for them. It seems as though, in heaven, there is no shortage of instruments of all kinds. There are also tutors here who talk lovingly to the children. It is a labour of love, recalling all the music that has ever been played, ever been thought of, ever been heard. It seems as though I am being drawn towards this wonderful sound. I hear choirs singing, (but I do not feel as if it is the 'angelic choirs' we were told, as children that we would see when we passed into spirit life and came to the 'pearly gates' where there would be someone with a halo for us and a pair of wings. No, my friend, there is no halo or pair of wings, there is only this light and this feeling of love and belonging that is here.) As I am with these children, I feel as if I am no stranger to them, as though I am as much a part of them as they are of me, and that every note of music is known to me. I feel it is like when you hear an old melody being played. I hear violins playing (I always did like violins) and I hear the singing – the sweet voices of the children and the deeper voices of those who are older. Yet there is no tremble in these voices although I see that the people who are singing are of a very great age range, from very young to very old. There is no loss of timbre in the quality of the voices. I feel strangely happy and content, as though my soul itself has been fed by the music.

My friend again looks at me and beckons. I follow and go outside again into the everlasting light that is here and see someone coming towards me. In the distance I recognise an old friend. I remember Grangemouth and the North and I feel an arm around me, holding me and grasping me as he did when he was on the earth plane – such a wonderful person! – a man who had so much to give his fellow man and who wanted to embrace everyone so that they would find what he had found in his life. Although he did not have much he was always full of understanding. As I am with him, I do not feel as though I need to call him by name, it is as though he knows my thoughts and I am as one with him and I think to myself how lucky I am to have met him again. I say 'Bill, forgive me, I did not manage to come to your funeral,' and he laughs and says, 'I didn't come to yours, either!' Somehow, it seems to us to be quite a huge joke because, I feel, how futile funerals are. Are we not still very much alive? He brings forth his favourite pipe and places it in his mouth and I am astonished that I had not thought of anything as normal as that. He says, 'It was a bad habit when I was on the earth plane and I feel very loathe to give it up. I do not smoke, but I still hold my pipe in my mouth so that I have the feel of security by doing so.' I thought to myself, 'I can understand why people still hold on to things that they thought, in their lifetime, was very much a part of themselves,' and I see that, one day, he will give up the pipe because he will feel that there is no need for it.

I ask of others who I was associated with when I knew him and he says, 'Well, some you will meet and some you will not meet, but that does not mean to say that they have not earned their place here.\You must never judge for yourself because it is not your judgement that is important.' He leaves the question open and I understand fully and do not ask any further. What is right for me to know at this particular moment of time will be given unto me and sufficient time will be given for everything.

I am quite pleased for myself at the progress I am making. I feel, at last, I am free to be able to live this experience and to understand. I still feel as though I would like to meet up with my family, and my friend looks and smiles and says, 'In a little while,' and I know that there is much that I must do first to earn the right to be able to be with them. I must accept myself as I was and as I am and not to worry over other people's opinions and faults. Too many of us, when we are in earth's life, think too much of what other people will do in set circumstances. We spend half of our life wasting our time, trying to avoid complications and other people's thoughts instead of living life to the full and finding God's understanding and love around us. Perhaps, to you who are in earthly life, it may seem as though it is a beautiful fairytale, but I say to you, that it is very real to me and I have found that there is more of God's thought made manifest to Man than Man will ever understand or comprehend.

I know that my life ahead now will become a beautiful thing and that I will be able to cope and to understand. I send thought out to my friend, 'When will I be able to write again?' and the thought comes back, 'When you have found true understanding of life here, then you will be given an opportunity.' I said to him, 'Well, no-one will ever read the book unless they are in spirit life,' and he smiled and said, 'We have ways and means of bringing many things about. When the time is right, you will be introduced to someone who will be able to help you – not from this side of life, but from the earth plane – someone who will act as your medium for you to control, for you to be able to bring forth truth.' I looked in amazement because I never, ever thought that perhaps, some time in the future, I would control someone who was considered sensitive enough to be used for contact from the spirit world. I began, then, to understand more fully the reason why I was brought to this library, to this music and to this understanding this day. I know that, if I am lucky, I will be able to write again through someone else and be able to bring light and truth and understanding of God's love to the earth people.

It seems so strange to say 'earth people' because it is as though there is a void between us, and yet there is no void. It is just a thought pattern a different vibration away. We are lighter in our thoughts and in our body structure than we were when we were in physical life, yet there is no difference in us in any way except that, here, we can find understanding, help and guidance from the ones who have gone into light for many years. They have been able to absorb that light and, by absorbing, become special people. Perhaps, one day, I will be permitted to become like these people. To be able to bring light to others; to be able to help to bring love to the dark corners of the universe; to be able to join with people who are of the same mind to bring about a spiritual revolution upon the earth plane – a revolution of thought. (I do not mean it in the military way, I mean that we will be able to find our own way, our own understanding).

I have looked and I have seen, upon the earth plane, the many changes that have happened. It seems as though I have not been here long and yet I know, in the passage of earth time, it has been quite some time and I feel an urgency with me. There is much that I should be doing. Again, my friend laughs. He smiles, nods his head and sends the thought to me, 'Sufficient for the day. Today has been very enlightening.' I have been able to listen to others in their endeavours to find beauty and light. I have been able to join with them and to think the same feelings as them – to find understanding. I wonder if, perhaps, one day, someone will pick up one of my books and be able to feel exactly as I feel at this moment of time – this lightness of heart and an eagerness to go forward and to progress.

No–one who is bathed in this light here would ever digress and go into darkness. Not unless there was purpose in mind, perhaps to help others who were in darker areas of thought. I feel as though my heart and soul are singing and I am content. I feel completely in attunement with everything here and I feel again that I shall be able to go forward and do much in the future to help those upon the earth plane who have a job to do. I say 'job' but it is not the word I would want to choose – there is a 'job' for us all to do, from the spirit side of life and from everyday life upon the earth, to bring forward God's truth and his understanding to those who are in ignorance and in need. To think, not of ourselves, but of our fellow man, to put ourselves in their position and then to find understanding and love for these people.

There is no need for worry over racial prejudice, nationalism or anything of that nature because, in God's light, when you are in the spirit world, you do not see the colour of a person's skin. I do not see a black skin or a white one, I just see a person. It is so strange! It is as though there is no nationality here. It is as though we are all at one with one another. As though, from the soul, all ego has been removed and all judgement of racial

thoughts and national thoughts. Only an essence is left – a pure
essence of love and understanding for each other. I wish that
when I was in earth life, I could have had a machine that could
sit someone down and bring them forward into full truth and
understanding. Then I realise that it is only by living that you
will ever find out the things that you have done right or wrong.
Your conscience must be your guide and the ones who are with
you from the spirit world must help you as well. As you wish
to progress, so they will help you to progress. So it is a
hand–in–hand business. It is one helping the other forward
towards light and I, in my turn, hope that I will be, in the
future, able to help others to see God's love.

CHAPTER 4

Of Things to Come

I see ahead of me much opportunity in the future (I know it may seem strange to say 'future'; yet even where I am, it is present with us) for me to be able to assimilate more knowledge and more understanding of people. If, when we were on the earth plane, we were more sensitive to other people's conditions of life, then we would truly be more open in our minds and there would be no need for conflict and trouble. We, in spirit life, are cushioned and helped in every way. I have felt no sadness or loss at leaving behind the earth life because I find now that what is here with me is stimulating to my thought and I am carried forward, ever with new thought being produced within my mind.

Today, I seem to be going forward at a very fast pace; and the one who is with me, walking beside me, beckons me on, as if to say, 'Hurry, or you will miss something.' I am wondering what it is that is so important that I should not miss it. Is it something that is a ritual, or is it something that only happens once in a while? But now I see a procession of children and they are laughing and happy and gay as though they are off on a picnic. I see baskets of food, and refreshments being carried by some. I also hear music, as though a band is playing and I hear grown-ups talking and joining in with the revelry. Then I realise that it is a Sunday School outing that I am seeing. In this place, of all places, a Sunday School outing! I look askance at the one who is beside me and he smiles and touches his nose as if to say, 'What is necessary for you to be shown will be shown unto you.' Then I begin to realise that these people are so set in the earth thoughts of their religion that they can give nothing up. That they must go on to follow the ritual and pattern that they made upon the earth plane, even though it is ridiculous to think of it in this place. I know we are steeped in religious teachings, but, here, religion is not a teaching, it is a way of life. It is the air you breathe, what you think, what you feel and what you see. There is no need for ritual and yet some must still carry on in the old plan, the old pattern. They cannot give it up. I feel saddened for them, although it seems to be a joyous occasion. I feel saddened for them, that their minds are not capable of rising above this and seeking knowledge. It is available for them here but they are staying in the same state of mind that they had on earth, following the rituals of the Church.

I go on now with my companion and we seem to be walking down a road that is getting dusty. It seems as though there is an acrid smell in the air; and I do not feel comfortable in this place. My companion begins to sense that I am uneasy and he sends thought towards me, 'Do not fear, I would not take you here if it was not right for you to come and see for yourself.' I am beginning to feel as though I am going towards a mine of some sort. I can smell sulphurous gases and I can see that there is a dank atmosphere here. I am surprised because I can see figures that seem to slouch and to drag one foot after the other, as though they have nowhere in particular to go. They seem just like the mouse in the cage that walks the treadmill – walking and running and going nowhere. I send thought out to my companion, 'What is this? Am I in hell?' and he says, 'There is no hell here, but this is the deepest darkness of Man's thought. Men who have not risen above conditions on the earth, who have not helped anyone, who have been utterly selfish and cruel in their manner and those who have, as we would say, sinned very badly. They are in this atmosphere because they cannot see beyond themselves.' There are beings of light I can see now as my eyes become accustomed to the gloom that seems to be around us, with this awful smell that seems to pervade the atmosphere. It is a 'bitterness' I smell and feel here, yet you see these beings of light moving around, tending and caring for these people and hoping that, perhaps, one day, they will put their hand out and ask for help. They cannot be helped until the soul realises for itself and looks toward light. Once the recognition of the soul has come, that person will see the being of light that is near him and he will hold out his hand and be helped.

I feel very saddened by these sights. I feel as though I am in a place that should not exist; but my companion sends a thought to me, 'This is not of God's making, but of Man's. Man's inhumanity to Man is made manifest here and it is a situation that will be until the time comes when Man has learned to overcome all the selfishness, the avarice and the greed that is with him, and truly turn in love to his fellow Man; to put his brother above himself in his own needs.'

Now my companion beckons me on and I seem to be coming into a less acrid atmosphere. The light seems to be pervading through and it is slightly brighter. I see that there are people moving now that seem to be lighter in their thought, because I am picking up their thought patterns and I hear them speaking to the ones that are working around them. I begin to realise that these souls have, at last, begun to understand and accept the need for light. So they are, at last, beginning on an upward path towards God's love and understanding. My companion smiles because he knows that I have realised the truth – that progression is open to all men and that God is merciful and is Love. Mercy and Love are all around us; even when we are in an earthly existence, there is always this love from our Father.

Perhaps it seems strange when you realise that God is not an earth man, as we in our concept of him tend to think, until we realise the energy that is here is from God. Then we begin to realise that Man, in his ignorance, is only a small part of the meaning of things. We have much to learn and understand. Man, in his ignorance, always thinks that he is the greatest thing that was ever created, and yet now I begin to realise how insignificant we truly are compared to the great manifestations of God's love and understanding for us.

Now I am coming out of this place, and the beautiful light envelops me. I feel bathed in a beautiful breeze that seems to take away all that has been around me in that atmosphere, as though the breeze has come to clear from me the smell and the feeling that was there. I send thought to my companion, 'How sad to think that Man can lower himself into an atmosphere like that because of bigotry and greed and lack of understanding for others.' He smiles and the thought comes to me, 'You see, they did not keep an open mind'; and I begin to realise how lucky I was, that my mind was always open to new ways of thinking and new ways of utilising thought.

Now the dusty road has disappeared and I see great edifices. I send thought, 'What can this be?' but, as soon as the thought has left my mind, it seems as though I have moved forward very fast and I am right by the door of one of these buildings. I am surprised, because I can hear the noise of industry and movement of machinery. I look at him and say, 'Well, why in God's heaven, is there a need of machinery?' He sends the thought, 'Inventors never stop inventing. You will never stop the ingenuity of Man's mind and the need to be able to put his hands to use.' I walk through and see these machines but I do not recognise them. They are like no machines I have seen on earth, yet they are doing work that is similar to machines that I have seen. These, however, seem to be far in advance. Again, my companion sends thought and says, 'These are the ones who will help the inventors of the future. The next generation that will go forth will be helped from spirit to find these machines and the knowledge to be able to use them. It is from spirit that great inspiration comes, even to the extent of composing music, writing books or anything of that nature. We, in spirit, send thought towards those on the earth plane but, sometimes, the thought is distorted by the person who is the recipient of the thought. We still have the human factor to overcome – Man's ego and Man's own control of his destiny. So some things that are invented for good are not used for good or, sometimes, inventions fail and yet we know, when we worked with them here that they were perfect in every way and should work. But I am afraid Man is not perfect, so the change occurs through his own power of thought.'

I go on through the building, absorbing all this wonderful knowledge, seeing the machines of the future. Then, I am afraid, because, as I go through this place, I see that, as the machines get bigger, so there is no need for Man to operate them. Then the realisation comes that, perhaps, progress will not be such a good thing because will it not cause unemployment and unrest amongst those who are not so well off? Those who, with time on their hands, would not be happy and would cause trouble and tribulation for those who were actively involved in occupation because they would not have the means to enjoy themselves in their spare time? They would be tense and angry beause of the loss that would be theirs with regard to the work promise for the future. Again, my companion looks at me and his mind pattern comes across. 'Yes, this is the difficulty for Man now. He must learn that, soon, his working time will be less than the time he has for relaxation. Now he must begin to realise that the people of the earth must be trained, not to work for their living, but to allow machines to work for them; and for them to find a way of utilising the other time (which will be great) to not cause trouble for others but to bring about a brotherly love and understanding for everyone else.' This was a very great lesson for me to learn, because it had not entered my head before that progress, in itself, can sometimes not be a good thing.

I have come through this place now and I seem to be leaving

by a different entrance. Again, I seem to be going from one building to another. Now I see such beautiful handicrafts, the colours of the wools and the silks in the tapestries that are being woven. I feel that I am not in the age that I was when I left the earth plane. It is as though I am coming towards a golden age – because the beauty that I see here is breath-taking. To realise that Man can create so much beauty. Then I begin to realise that each tapestry is telling a story.

It seems to be a history of the earth – not kept for one country or another – but I see it interwoven. Then I begin to realise fully what this is. It is the pattern of Man joining his hands across sea and land, helping another country in difficulty. I see patterns there that change, and I realise this is when there has been a great upheaval, such as the First World War. I can see the patterns of countries joining hands to resist another and I do not like to gaze upon this because the colours seem strident; as though the military mind has taken over even on this tapestry of life. Then I see the times of peace and children playing in the fields. I see the flowers growing, the corn ripening. It seems to be moving. I see the future and it seems as though this could be wonderful; yet I see that, by the side of the one who weaves, there are these dark colours again and I think, 'Oh, could not Man, now, learn a lesson and put aside from this person who creates this life tapestry the need to bring in the dark colours which mean more trial and tribulation.' I pray that Man, in his ignorance, will find light and truth and understanding with his fellow Man; that there will be no need for this tapestry of life to ever change from anything that is beautiful.

It has given me much thought when I consider the waste of Man's life – to be cut short, to be used in such a manner that it brings no joy to God, that youth of all countries should be utilised to cause destruction to each other. I feel sad and I send thought about, 'Perhaps, one day, the statesmen of each country will begin to realise fully the true meaning of life's tapestry – that men should help each other and progress; that each one should put his shoulder to the plough to help another in times of trouble; that, when there is famine in one country, other countries will send grain and love, understanding and help; and, when great tragedies come, such as eruptions from volcanic structures and earthquakes, others will think of and send comfort to these people.' There will be enough for Man to do, just helping each other through the natural disasters that come, without making disasters and without spoiling what is the true potential – that Man should live the best he can, to bring about a heaven on earth.

Perhaps, one day, Man will be able to overcome his baser instincts and will truly progress. Then the future may be bright for the children of all lands so that all will be fed, all will be clothed and all will be happy with each other; living in unison under the great light of God. I know, as I am thinking this, that it will take a great miracle to bring it about, but perhaps small miracles will occur which will make man think beyond himself. Then, as these miracles join together, they will, in essence, form the size of the miracle that will be needed for Man to live in peace with his fellow Man.

With reflective thought, I begin to realise the true significance and the workings of God's kingdom. I begin to realise that some of the sayings in the Bible, although archaic, are true in some aspects, although they have been changed with the passage of time. The words, 'In my Father's house, there are many houses.' In my Father's kingdom there are many places for people to be. I realise fully that it is what you do upon the earth plane that fashions your life in this life. It is the continuance of your mind patterns that formulates the place you will stay. How you have lived on earth and how you have behaved is the most important thing in the structure of your new life. Those who have loved and those who have been kindly, even if they have been of poor means, are sometimes more greatly rewarded than those who have done many great things. It is simplicity of mind, the love of your fellow Man and the love of your Father, God, that are the most important factors of all.

Many people, when they are in earth life, will do nothing unless there is something in it for themselves – some reward, some furtherance of their ambitions – that can be brought about in the use of doing something for someone else. But it is the ones who have given themselves freely to others, who have sacrificed their own feelings to help others, such as the daughter who has sacrificed the chance of marriage to look after elderly parents and then, by the time the parents have passed into spirit, it has been too late for her and yet she felt no bitterness, feeling that she had done her duty to her parents and that she would not have changed things, even if she could have. It is the unselfish act of someone who will lay down his life for his friend; or someone who sees the need of someone else in need, so that, even though he is hungry himself, he would give his food away to someone else. Many such incidents have been seen in the past through many generations, and it is these unselfish acts that are the most important factors of all. I wish, in my life span, I had had more knowledge of after-life.

It seems as though everyone shuns the word 'death'. People are all afraid of it because it sounds so final. They see the picture of the grim reaper coming with the scythe across his shoulder in skeleton form to meet them and they are afraid. They do not see that it is not so. That the hands of the ones who have passed on before, the loved ones who have truly loved and cared for you in past life, wait for you to come. There is no grim reaper, there is no-one standing at the gates dishing out to people halos and harps and beautiful voices so they can be in the heavenly choir. It is a fallacy, my friend. The reality is as though you have just passed from one room to another and it is a continuation of life. True, it is on a lighter vibration and you are not restricted by body ailments or by ties of family but, even with this lightness, there is a responsibility. Even in the life you lead after you pass into spirit, you are still personally responsible for your actions. That is continual, it does not stop when you pass into spirit life. Being in spirit does not mean that you are no longer responsible for anything and that you can, if you have behaved yourself enough to be in a good sphere of living, do just the same things as you would want to do and not care. There is a continual progression. There are many who leave the earth and say, 'I never want to come to earth again.' They do not realise that they have to earn the right to be able to come to earth again; or that they have to earn the right to remain in spirit life; or to earn the right to help another medium by becoming a teacher. You see everything is progression. No-one stays still. As you go forward in spirit life and earth life, so there are daily lessons to be learnt and I, even now, am learning lessons with each day that passes. (I say 'day' because to me it is another day, another dawn, but there is no actual dawn or day or dusk, it is continual time.)

There is always this beautiful, mellow, golden light about us. There is always this feeling of love and understanding. There is always this kindness of thought towards each other because we are well aware of each other's needs and feelings; and then there is always the thought towards the ones who pass into spirit. The ones who have a long time to wait to grow up, to be fully understanding of their situation and the help that comes from those who join with them to help them through this period of time so that they are not anxious for the ones they have left behind. You see how wonderfully it affects people. You see people when they first come; when they seem to be tired and weary from their earth life. Then it is as though they shed earth years and return to a younger period of life, where they had more vitality and it is as though they have gained this extra strength, this extra vitality, to be able to enjoy the situation in which they now find themselves.

Then, gradually, they begin to realise that they are fortunate in the sphere they are living in. What can they do to help others who have not found themselves so fortunate when they pass into spirit life? You see, the conscience is there, the conscience that says: 'I must help my brother, I must go and help him or her to be able to come forward into light.'

This is how it is, it is eternal progress. No thought for oneself, but thought for ones who are not quite as fortunate. Thought for ones who are still left upon the earth plane, who are still struggling and not able to see their way clear through the fog of life and difficulties that are around them. Then they draw close to the earth and try to contact those who are in the position to be able to act as a bridge between the two worlds. Then they are able to communicate in services of clairvoyance to their people, or by trying to make them understand in their home environment by the moving of objects. By the whispers of love into the ear of the one they wish to contact. So, you see, there is always this thought of other people, not selfish thought, and that is important. It is so easy, when you are in earth life, to be selfish, to think to yourself, 'Oh, nobody else knows. I can do this and get away with it.' It is so easy to do this, to fall into this way of thinking, but, my friend, that is one of the most cardinal sins of all. To be selfish and utilise situations to suit yourself, and not to care about other people's feelings and the consequences of your actions. So you, who are left on earth, I hope that when you read the words that I have brought forward, you will understand and try, whilst you are still in your earth environment, to achieve more, perhaps, than I did. That, with a little fore-knowledge, you will be able to find more understanding.

To keep an open mind is essential; to realise that there are greater wonders in the world and in the heavens than Man can ever comprehend. Do not shut your mind off and stick to a religious dogma, but think to yourself: Jesus preached in the hills. He went everywhere on foot and did not have anyone to help him, only his disciples who followed him with love and understanding. He knew their frailties of mind and he helped and strenghtened them and, as he went on his way, he did nothing that would harm anyone else. He just treated everyone as an equal, regardless of their station in life. This is how, truly, we should be with one another. We should not care what assets these people have, whether they are brilliant mathematicians or brilliant doctors, or clergymen, or just an ordinary person who is working in an everyday environment, trying very hard to make ends meet. They are all equal in God's eyes. No man is greater than another. When you can begin to realise this, my friends, then, truly, you are becoming as God would wish you to be.

CHAPTER 5

God's Love Made Manifest

Again, it seems to be the start of another day. The light filters through to me and I begin to wonder whether it is days that are passing or a much longer period of time. It is so measureless here, and it seems to be that you are able to achieve much in such a short space of time. I see my friend awaiting me and, again, he smiles (he is such a pleasant person to be with, it fills me with joy and happiness just to be in his presence) and he leads the way that I am to travel this time.

As we go along the road, I feel his mind talking to me again. He is talking about the hospitals that are in spirit and of the need for such institutions. I feel a little bewildered at this because, after all, are we not past the need for doctors and nurses? He sends a thought to me that there are many people who do not realise that, when a person passes from a long illness into spirit life, there is need for an adjusting period of time. This helps the soul into the recognition that they have passed over, and have made the transition from one life pattern to another.

So I go quite happily with him towards what seems to me to be a place of happiness. Everything is light and bright and the uniforms that the nurses are wearing (because I can see them) are of translucent colours. They are neither one colour or another. They seem to be many hues blended together to make such a delicate shade that it is not hurtful to the eyes. I can see that the only way you can distinguish between them is by the different shapes of caps that they wear – reminiscent, a lot, of nurses attire upon the earth plane – yet I see some whose uniforms are quite different, and I pick up the thought that this is future wear for nurses. As though they are, even in this capacity, adjusting life ahead for people who are in that position upon the earth plane.

I see that there are many patients in beds, but they seem to be hovering above the beds, as though they are not actually lying on them. It seems as though they have an air space between them and the bed. It is a very funny thing to realise that, although they are lying in a horizontal position, they are not actually touching the bed. He sees me look and smile and sends the thought to me, 'You must remember that some patients are very bad with bed sores when they leave your earthly life and, until they finally adjust to this life, they still expect to have the pain from these things. Also, the etheric body does not need to rest on anything. It is, as you would say, a figment of the imagination of the patient.' I see that some are in a deep sleep and some seem to be awake, yet not awake, as though they have had drugs and are just beginning to adjust to coming out of the influence of these drugs. The thought comes to me, 'Ah, yes, because they are in different stages of this development from the transition to full realisation of their passing.' I send thought to him ; 'Well, what of the children and of the ones who die a sudden death in an affray or war?', and he sends thought back to me, 'If we stay here long enough, you will see what happens.'

It is almost as though it is an immediate reaction to the thought, for I see, suddenly, the forms of the nurses start to be more efficient, more bustling, as though they are preparing for some new arrivals. Suddenly I see ambulances drawing up to the entrance of the building and porters going forth with movable stretchers to assist the ambulancemen to off-load the people that they have brought. I realise now, as I look, that what I am seeing is the result of what would be called, in your earth term, a pile-up on the motorway. These people have all been injured or killed in foggy road conditions and ice and are being brought through now to be helped. I see the bewilderment on some of their faces and the anxiety. I hear a tentative whisper, 'Please, can you tell my daughter?'. She does not realise that her daughter has already been informed, not of her safe arrival into hospital, but that she has slipped away into a different life – one where she will feel no more pain. I see beyond this person to a young girl crying, and I begin to realise then, that when we are on the earth plane and we cry for our loved ones whom we have lost, we do not realise that even our tears can penetrate into the heavenly spheres. Now I understand fully what people have meant when they have said to me, 'Your tears will hold back the progression of your loved one,' because if this woman was adjusted into full knowledge, she would hear her daughter's anguish and would be saddened as she would not be able to join her and to comfort her.

I see them being placed into comfortable positions. I see the look of confidence in the faces of the ones who are receiving treatment, as though they know they are in good hands; and I see doctors going, in pairs, from one bed to another, talking to them and putting them at their ease. Then I see a little farther on, and I see a quiet act of sedation for them, to help with the shock that they have sustained. With some, I see that there is a greater degree of shock than with others, and my companion sends thought to me, 'These people will be given extra help.' He beckons me across the ward, through into the hallway and along a long corridor with many doors with name-plates and instructions on them. I hear the noise of instruments and metallic things being moved, then I am in a room in which there is a great machine with a glass dome that fits over the top – almost like a glass compartment – and I see one of these people being brought forward and placed in this compartment Then, as the glass dome closes over the patient, I see a brilliant blue light begin to descend, as though it comes from the ceiling down through the glass, and it looks to me as though the whole glass is a blue bubble of light. I can see the recumbent form of the patient there and I can see that, at last, he is at peace. There is no movement or anguish about him but it seems as though he is completely enveloped in this light. I am engrossed in watching because I have never witnessed anything like it or ever thought that anything like this could possibly be used. Then the treatment is finished and the light recedes. The glass dome opens and, when I look at the face of the person who was placed there, I see that all the lines and wrinkles are gone from the face and this man looks 20 years yonger than the man who was placed in the machine. It is as though the light has had a rejuvenating effect upon him and he seems to me to be completely replenished in every way, except that he is sleeping peacefully like a child.

I walk past him lying there and through a door because my companion is beckoning me and drawing me forward. I go into another ward which, if I was on the earth plane, I would say was a psychiatric ward – a ward where there are patients who seem to be in need of extra help and care. I send thought towards my companion because I feel the love and compassion in this place building up, almost to a crescendo. It seems as though the love is turning into different colour rays that seem to be bombarding us as we walk into this ward-like atmosphere. I see that there are many young ones here, and old, all together. There is no segregation of the sexes. They seem to be happy and content with each other and they are doing things that, I would say, would be therapeutic for them to be able to adjust. I see someone weaving a basket and someone doing embroidery. It seems strange to me to see a man doing embroidery, yet I feel that there are many people who are gifted in this way. My companion sends thought to me again, 'These are people who, unfortunately, have been hurt by others; people who have passed into spirit violently at the hands of someone else.' I look and I see no fear with them. I see a calmness and an adjustment to their area of living. I see that they are quite content with the area they are in, and he sends thought to me, 'They will not be here for long. They will soon be fully adjusted and will integrate into the community life here.' I think, 'How wonderful! We do not realise that people are cared for and loved so much.'

In that atmosphere, it felt as if the very air that you breathed was love and understanding and I could see how they needed this because of the nature of their passing. I send thought to my companion, 'It seems terrible that people will hurt others so', and he sends thought back, 'You must remember that Man is one of the most ferocious and cruel animals upon the earth plane because he will deliberately kill his own species. He will not only do it because of hunger or need, but because of anger or greed.' Then I began to realise more fully that Man, himself, can be very selfish and unfeeling for others and I felt saddened in my heart that these things could come to pass. With such a love as God has given us, such an understanding of all things, such a wonderful place to live in – the world and all it's creations of life there, the manifestations of love in family life (a mother's love for her child, a grandmother's love for her grandchild, and people's love for their animals) – it did not seem possible that Man could be very evil and be low in his thoughts, but again the thought came to me, 'You must remember that there are two selves in Man. A higher and a lower self. If a man leads a proper life, the higher self is made manifest but, if he becomes degenerate and selfish, his moods become ugly and he assumes the role of the lower self. Then he gradually deteriorates in his thoughts and mind until he is able to do things to others that, normally, if he was (as you would say) in his right mind, he would not do.'

You see, again, God's given gift of freedom of will comes into everything. On all levels and aspects of life it is Man's conscience that should be the ruling light of his life, but how many of us, when we are on the earth plane, close our ears to that small voice within us which is the guiding light between right and wrong.

I am now leaving this atmosphere because I feel very sad to realise that Man has much to learn and there is much that we, from spirit, can do to enlighten others. I send thought to my companion, 'When can I be used to help others? It is very interesting for you to show me these wonderful aspects of spiritual life, but when will I be able to help others?' He looks at me and, again, a smile comes with the thought, 'When the time is right and you have accepted all the lessons that are here for you to see. You must see Man's inhumanity to Man and you must understand that these things can be overcome by good thought. Light can always overcome darkness and, even if someone is travelling on a wrong road, you can always pray for them.' I say to you who are still upon the earth plane: Pray for those who would use you wrong; pray that they will find God's light and understanding so that their lives will become enriched, that they will be able to fulfill their rightful place upon the earth; to live their lives in an exemplory manner; to be able to be of use to their fellow man; to bring about, throughout the world, a better way of life, of caring for one another; to do away with strife and anger. It will take many centuries for this. Perhaps it will never be achieved but, unless you all try, unless you put your heart with your thoughts and think unselfishly of others, nothing will ever be achieved.

Your Father was wise. He knew your thoughts. He knew that you were weak and that you needed strength and His love is the strengthening factor. His love and His light descend towards all Mankind. There is no difference in His love for a black man or a white one because, to Him, all are equal. So I say to you: Do not be pious and think that you are good and better than others – be humble and, in your humility, go forward in light and truth. Let not your lives be coloured by untruths and bad thought. Put aside your own objectives for greed and advancement and think of others. Help one another when in need. Do not hurt one another physically or by feelings. Put aside all thoughts of anger. Find goodness in each other. Look not for the bad things but only for the good and you will find that, in each of us, there is a little good. If there is not a lot, at least the seed is there and, if it is watered with love and human kindness, then it will grow so that it will become a beautiful flower – a beautiful plant – and it will continue to grow and it will be able to pollinate other people's thoughts and minds so that in them the seed will grow.

As I look out from where I am onto other planes of understanding, I begin to realise that behind God's laws there is a great humanity, a great love and understanding. The ones who are in spirit, who draw close to us many times, are truly bathed in the same thought and they bring towards us our Father's love for us. Think not of God as a kindly old man, but think of him as the life-giving force of everything in creation. A power beyond all comprehension, light and love and everything that is beautiful; a feeling that you are being looked after and understood in every way.

Here my friends, you have no outer garment of life to cloak your thoughts. Here, you are bare to the very soul and yet, as you look at one another, you feel this love penetrating everywhere. You feel as though you are a king to eveyone and you do not feel lonely, even if you have not yet met up with your loved ones as I, myself, have yet to do. You do not feel as though you are lost, You feel as though you completely belong with everyone here; as though, if you used your mind, you could use their mind because you are so alike in thought.

It is a wonderful feeling to know that everyone is linked, that everyone is important. How many times, upon the earth plane, do people feel as though, if they died tomorrow, no-one would miss them? if they had a tragedy tomorrow, no-one would help them? and, if they were hungry, they would starve alone? I say to you: Think well on my words. Look about you in your plane of life and realise that it is by your own individual actions that you, yourself, are judged and that you do have time to help others. Even if you have no money, you can help by being kind and understanding; by showing love to someone who is lonely; by helping a child when it falls; and by making sure that someone who is old and frail has no reason to be afraid of the strength of others. You will find that in your own children and the children of others, there is a pent-up feeling of frustration that seems to grow, but you, by your examples, must show to them that there is more beyond the earth life; that material things and racialism count for nothing but that universal love for one another is the most important factor of all. You will find that if you can generate love to others, love will be generated to you in return.

CHAPTER 6

Inspiration

How many dawns have I seen and recognised since coming into this new life, and yet the passage of time does not worry me or interfere with me or my thoughts in any way. I feel no yearning or longing to see my loved ones. I know that when the time is right they will appear to me, but I am content to wait until it is the right time because then I shall know instinctively that all is well. It is a time of blessedness, a time of peace of mind. I am able to look upon the horizon and see the beauty of God's creation – even more expansive than on the earth plane – even more beautiful! Here, the flowers do not seem to break up and die. You never see a petal fall from a rose. The rose remains intact and then, one day, it is no longer there but is replaced by another – equally as beautiful. There is no decay, no sense of loss here. There is this wonderful feeling of being bathed in love and understanding. There is this wonderful joy within one's soul to realise and to recognise the beauty of God's love and his manifestation of it towards all Mankind.

I have met with many troubled souls who have come into spirit life not knowing what to expect. I join with people and talk to them and I find that their preconceived ideas on earth are totally ambiguous – they do not tally with what we are experiencing now. We are able to think together, and to think of many controversial subjects that, when on earth, would have caused arguments and strife. Here it is a case of being fair and not being critical, but listening to both sides and then to formulate your own opinion quietly and with understanding.

I see people who, I know, when on earth, were of different races, creeds and colours and yet, here, (it is so strange), you do not recognise the colour of a person's skin, only the beauty of the soul within. It is a pity that Man, whilst he is struggling on earth, cannot know the wonderful love that is there inside his brother man, even if his skin is not of the same colour or if he does not share the same cultural background. It is so sad to think that we have to wait until we have reached spirit life before we can really appreciate the love that should be within us for each other. There are many now, in earth life, who think nothing of each other but only strive for power. Their ambition carries them along on the crest of a wave, but it is not a gentle wave – it is a tidal wave that will sweep much trouble upon the earth!

Man must understand his fellow man while there is still time. There must be an end to racial prejudice, even if we do not fully understand one another. Even if, after we integrate, there are still some differences of opinion. Well, is it not right for people to have differences of opinion and yet be able to be in harmony with one another? It would not be good for all of us to be of the same opinion, the same thought. It would not do for all of us to want to lead the same lives. There will be some whose lives are quite uneventful, quite unmeaning because the quality of the soul has not yet reached a stage where they would seek more in this life. Then you have the great ones who are natural philosophers. They do not realise that they are spirit-guided. They feel as though the great wisdom that is within them is of their own knowledge, of their own seeking in great books of knowledge. They do not realise that it is simply put there so that, when the need arises, the thought is there, ready to manifest.

It is the same with the beautiful music that pervades the atmosphere and comes to earth. Some young man, who will be named a genius, hears haunting melodies being played from the spirit realms and jots these few notes down on paper. Then he reaches for a piano and begins to extemporize on the melody that comes through, and the beauty of it starts to grow and it becomes HIS creation. It is so strange that he does not realise that someone in spirit life spread this knowledge to him because they knew he had the beauty of mind to be able to place that melody with other notes so that it would become a thing of beauty and not just a haunting thing going off on a vapour of air.

So you see, my friends, even the painters suddenly get an inspiration. They must draw something or someone — there is a haunting quality about the face of this young girl or that old man – something that is there in the character of the person – and they feel impelled to put it onto canvas, They do not realise that there is some force that is impelling them to use their talent to bring about the creation of the beautiful painting that will result. They do not realise that, although they may sweat or starve, the creativity that is being used through them is something that comes – to the musician, as a haunting melody – to the painter a beauty in someone's old and tired face, or that of a young child who is full of innocence and no guile.

Then we come to the ones who feel they want to put pen to paper. They want to write somthing inspiring; something to alter the whole pattern of the earth; something that will give someone a chance to think for themselves, to be able to start to seek for more knowledge. So they sit down and suddenly, from the pen, there arrives this wonderful book. Then it is signed by the person who has written it – but did they truly write it or was there not someone, a counterpart in spirit, who worked in unison with that person to bring about the creation of that wonderful knowledge?

Then we come to the orator – the man who has magic in his voice; the man who can hold an audience spellbound. He only has to stand there and to look, and already they are captured.

Then he starts to talk and they cannot tear themselves away from one single word. Such a beauty in the words and the way in which they are put forth reaches into the soul of Man and brings about a larger understanding of things. This also comes from the world of spirit towards Mankind. It is someone who, with great knowledge and a great store of philosophy, wishes to make an impact into the present-day conditions of the world and so he choses an instrument which he feels is fitting to the employment (or job, as you would say), and so that young man is elected and suddenly comes out to the fore because he can speak and hold people with his knowledge. Again, it is not his knowledge, just a fleeting thing – but something that comes on the ethers of light towards him as he stands and walks about in his daily life. So you can see that throughout the creation of Man and his understanding there is always extra knowledge that is being fed through.

Then we have the doctor who is just a simple man – one who has worked with children or has led a country life – visiting people in outlaying farms, no matter what time of the day or night, because of the dedication that is within him. But it is a dedication that is filled with love for his fellow man. He is able to be used as an instrument so that that love can be manifested in such a way that it will bring about a relief of the sickness and the illness of Mankind.

Then we have the nurse – someone who has to wash and change someone if they are in difficulties. Or pehaps someone has to be spoon-fed, so the nurse goes and puts her arm around the person and says, 'Come on, my dear, I'll help you'.

Then we have those who do the menial jobs. The ones who, perhaps, only wash the floors and help in other ways. But they, too, are inspired with a great love, a great happiness within themselves, content to remain in the background of things as long as they can be of service. So it should be with the ones who take office – to bring forward the great knowledge of

God. It should not be a thing that is because of an exam they take. It should be that they have taken their exams through life, through experience, through love of their fellow man so that, when they come to the time when they feel that they are dedicated enough to continue further, to take the mantle of a priest, or curate, or vicar, or even someone who is only a sidesman in the church, to have the dedication within themselves to know that the love inside them is so great that they could not live their daily lives unless they were acting in service for Him, our Father, God.

So you see these people go forth. The ones who look after the lepers; the ones who are working with children who are suffering from terminal illnesses; ones who give comfort to the old who are in need before they pass from this life into a higher life. These people are not only dedicated, but are guided by spirit, they are helped, they are shown light and the light builds within them and manifests the rays of love that God, himself, sends to earth. These rays are filtered through the people who gain dedication and they are transmuted into something more powerful, more beautiful than just light. They are love, manifested upon the earth – the power of God, manifested towards Man with mercy and love and understanding.

There are also those, unfortunately, who, in their daily lives, lead selfish lives. They see nothing beyond their material needs, wants or considerations. They do not think of the suffering of the ones around them. As long as they have food upon their table – something to eat and drink, a 'a little in the bank', a car to ride backwards and forwards in – they do not think of others who, perhaps, have nothing; who do not know where their daily bread will come from unless they go quietly on their knees to their Father, God and say: 'Dear God, help us this day'. There have been many who have had nothing, who, by prayer alone, have been sustained upon the earth. There have been many wonderful people who have had the care of children in their hands; children from the poorer communities of life who have nothing, not even a change of shoes or clothes. These people dedicate themselves to the growth of the souls of those children so that, even if they cannot give them monetary things and assets, at least they can help to build their characters and to fill their souls with love. It is to the dedication of these people that I would like to bring your attention. The ones who give selflessly to others; the ones who care not for their own suffering or the burdens of their life, but only for how they can help someone in need. I always remember the parable of the Samaritan. How many times in life have we noticed that it is not always our friends who stand by us so staunchly when we are in need or in difficulty or trouble? It is sometimes a stranger who seems to appear on the horizon and comes towards us to extend the hand of friendship and give gentle advice and help. Have there not been many times, when someone has had an accident or there has been a bereavement in the family, when suddenly someone arrives – someone they had not known previously but somehow knows their needs and is there to extend that help? You see, all these people are spirit guided, are helped by the ones who send love from after-life through to bring forward the true humility and humanity of man.

Then you have those who work with the animals. I am sad to say that there is much that is done in the name of progress to our friends, the beasts of the fields and the household pets, who are taken and used in vivisection. A beastly, terrible situation! After all, all they want is to serve us in the capacity that they are capable of – a dog to give his friendship; a cat to purr and to be pleased to see you; also the sturdy horse who would ride himself into the ground if you only gave him the command; the gentle beasts of the field – the cows, the pigs, the chickens and the ducks and all the smaller creatures – they all expect Man to treat them with love, but I am afraid it is not so. There are many who have much to answer for when they return to spirit life because of how they have treated God's creatures – those who cannot speak for themselves, those who serve dumbly, those who are loving in their own way, and gentle.

So, my friends, there is much to understand. There is much to look to and to listen for. There are many things that Man will never comprehend in his ignorance. But God knows of his ignorance and sends light filtering through the atmosphere so that there can be new music created, new thought created, new love manifested. This, in itself, is a wonderful thing – to think that his love reaches out to us, although we may be as the sands on the shore. There may be millions of grains, who knows. It is a wonderful thing when you realise how marvellous His contact with us is, how great the love for us that is there, and the light. On the earth plane, we are pleased when it becomes summer, so that we can shed clothing and feel the kiss of the sun. Again, on a dark night, is it not a lovely friendly feeling when the moon comes out to light your way? But so much more light comes from your Father, God towards you. The light of understanding. Understanding your weaknesses and your fears; understanding, truly, that there is something beyond comprehension, and that a Man can alter his whole life by just rising above himself and keeping to the higher self instead of the lower.

It is a wonderful thing. God knew exactly what he was doing when he created us. He knew exactly the duplicity of Man in his mind – how he would scheme, how he would behave in set circumstances – and yet, even then, he gave freedom of will. Freedom knowing full well that Man would chose to go on his own pathway of life and would not always take the path of right but would take the path that leads to the alteration of the beauty of life. God, in his wisdom, knew that, by giving Man this freedom of will, he was also helping to create another force which would be opposite to light but he, in his fairness, realised that Man must learn for himself. So, as we go through life, we are taught many lessons and, as we go through after-life, there are more lessons to come. But, my friends, this love from out Father is always manifesting towards us and he gives us peace of mind in his understanding.

We are children of his thought and were created. We must always remember that our place upon the earth with the animals is a sacred trust; that we are entrusted to care for them and to look after them properly. It is about time that Man shouldered his responsibilities.

CHAPTER 7

Of Human Bondage

We have heard this phrase used in many ways before but never did I realise, until I had passed into the world of spirit, the bondage that human beings make of their lives and of their souls. How they become so enmeshed in material considerations that they cannot see beyond these things and so they do not see the light of God around them. They do not understand. They live in such narrow channels of thought that they never see beyond, are never able to enlighten themselves or to help others. They just have their own selfish aims and their own greedy ways. When it is time for them to pass into spirit, they cannot understand why, suddenly, they are transported into a totally different way of life, and they cannot leave these thoughts behind. They bring the thoughts with them so their atmosphere, instead of being light and airy and beautiful, is weighed down with the bondage of these thoughts.

Their progression is a thing that is practically non-existent because of their own ways and thoughts. They cannot see beyond to the love that is manifested towards them from the beings in spirit. All they are worried about is the loss of their immediate material considerations and so, with their minds, instead of seeing beautiful things growing, they gather to themselves the means to make their life as it was, in thought. They care not for the consideration of others because, in their own way, they were selfish and mean. So, they walk about in a fog and they can see no further than their noses with regard to the spiritual aspect of life.

Then you have the ones who have been bigots upon the earth; those who have been so sure of their own importance; those who have practised their religion from the pulpits, bringing forward God as someone who was wrathful. The children of this wrathful God still, in their own way, expect to find 'hell and brimstone' and so, you see, their mind conjures up the picture of 'hell and brimstone' so they are immersed in their own hell – a hell of their own making!

Then you get the simple soul – the one who has seen no wrong in others; the one who has led a simple, generous way of life, giving of their own things to others, their own thoughts and, by their deeds, helping those in need. Their lives are totally different because, in their minds, there is beauty. So the beauty becomes a thing of reality and they are placed in situations where there is a lovely garden and a lovely little house where they can rest assured with peace of mind.

So you could say that the spirit world is, in some ways, a figment of Man's imagination, but it is really the soul being able to transmute the thoughts of Man and put them into a spiritual perspective. The simple people are ones who have had open minds; ones who have always been generous in their way of life with other people, giving of themselves regardless of what strain it caused in their own lives. Ones who have sacrificed many things for others, who have, perhaps, given up their lives to help their parents because they had no-one else to help them do so; ones who have given of themselves in true vocation of work, in nursing in the hospitals and looking after the sick people. The doctors who are of an older breed, who gave of themselves willingly, who walked for miles across moors to get to patients when the horse would not go or the car broke down.

These people who, in their lives, were generous to others, find that their own lives were filled with generous thoughts that are being sent back to them. Love is being given to them by the ones that are in spirit to reward them for what they gave to others so their lives become beautiful and they are able to see the true meaning of God's heaven. They see the wonderful light around them. They see the beautiful, clear crystal waters. They see the flowers that never seem to fade, the beauty that is always there, the strength in the trees, the rarified air in the hills. They begin to see this as, really, a heaven, and they begin to realise how much God's love is meant for them.

Again, we think of the ones who are enmeshed in their own thoughts and we feel sorry for them because we know that they have reached their limitations and they will find it very difficult to open themselves towards light. This is when the beings of light – who work regardlessly here, who help others in many capacities – go into their regions and spend eons of time just being there, hoping that these people will see light and will be able to be helped. They do not care for themselves, they work regardless of thought for themselves, just giving light in these dark places.

Man, in his foolishness, has made his own bondage. He has made his own way, his own hell. But we will go forward from these thoughts now towards the ones who will take near-future life. The ones who are being prepared to return to the earth plane; to return, again, to human bondage – the bondage of being housed into a human body so that the soul is imprisoned and held in place, so that the soul, itself, cannot progress in the manner it would like to but must wait for events to happen so that it can begin to shine and refurbish itself.

I am in a chamber now where there are many souls gathered. It is like being in university because there is a tutor and the pupils. They are all listening very attentively to the lectures that are going on. These lectures go on for days and days on many aspects and many things because they are being taught the future and not the past. They are being shown the way that their lives will evolve in the span of life that they will face now upon the earth plane. They are being shown all aspects of life – how the development of Man will go and God's pattern for Man's development is being spread out before them. They are being shown the technology of the new age. They are being brought truly up to date with everything that will be in their life cycle plan. So you see, my friends, before people go to earth to become human people, they are given full instructions, they are able to cope. How many times have we said of the new generations to come: How will they ever be able to cope with the way of life that is going to be – the violence and the upsetting thoughts that will be manifested in their lives? Yet, my friends, they are well prepared. They have taken their degree in spiritual life and they are well prepared for the resumé of human life.

Then I am permitted to go further. My friend, who comes to stand by my side, beckons me on into a place which I would say was like an incubator because I am seeing the souls as they truly are now that they are without the shapes and forms that I had seen before. The etheric shapes have been taken away and I am seeing the nucleus of the souls. I am seeing all different stages of development. I am seeing some which are almost, to me, pure gold, and I am seeing others that are very small, who have patches of darkness upon them, as though they are tarnished. My companion smiles at me and sends thought, 'Do you often wonder how much your soul has progressed, and whether it shines or is dull?' I send thought to him, 'At this moment of time, I would rather not know'.

Then I see that these souls are waiting now for the time when the parents will be together and the love that is between them will bring about the blessing of a new event in their lives and I think, 'I wonder if I will ever again walk on earth. Will I ever earn the right to be able to go back and try to bring about more knowledge and more understanding of God's true work through spirit to the earth?'.

I leave this place and I feel elated because I feel as though each generation will be able to cope; will be able to manage in the years ahead. Where I, as a person on earth, have despaired about the future and future generations, now I know that there is no need to despair because here is the truth – the nucleus of life – and I am being shown it from the very beginning, the first cycle of birth. I am extremely privileged to have been shown this because in Man's concept of thought, he cannot accept, in many ways, the thought of reincarnation. Yet, with simplicity of mind, you begin to realise that you could not possibly, in one lifetime, absorb all knowledge. So there must be a regeneration of the mind and of the soul.

Now I am going from this chamber out into the gloom that seems to be pervading the atmosphere. I look askance towards the one who is my companion: 'I do not see souls in need here and yet there is a gloom.' He sends thought to me, 'This is the twilight hour before regeneration of the soul, and they are conditioned to the atmosphere that they must return to – the heavier atmosphere of human life and the earth plane. These souls must be gradually accustomed to the different levels that they will go through before they reach the level of earth life.' Then I begin to wonder. I didn't realise how much difference there is between the planes of light and the plane of earth, and that there was this heaviness we came through towards light. Now these children who will go forth into human life must return through the darker atmosphere to earth life. It seemed to me such an easy step, but I did not realise how lucky I was to awake with full realisation of my surroundings. I realised how privileged I had been to be given help and to have an open mind. I look at these little souls and I think to myself, 'I wonder who they will be. Will there be another Einstein? Will there be another Rachmaninov? Will there be another Keiser or Hitler?' Until they have gone through earth life we will not know.

Into each generation there comes good as well as evil because Man must learn to rise above himself, above the baser instincts of himself, so that he can become a spiritual being. It is such a shame to think that the workings of God can be mutilated in such a way that evil can manifest itself, but you must always remember that where there is good, there is bad. Where there is light, there is dark; where there is love, there is hate. It is a thing that we must learn in our own lives – to find a balance. We, ourselves, as souls, must learn to find light instead of darkness. This, in itself, is a great lesson of life. The light that manifests from God is so great, but it is too rich for the atmosphere of earth and so it must be just an essence of God's love that comes through the atmosphere towards the earth plane and Man will never truly, when he walks the earth, find the full realisation of God's love for him. It is only when you come into spirit life and see the workings of the ones who work in unison together to perpetrate the work of the Father, that you see how they bring this light forth so that Man can evolve.

My companion picks up my thoughts and the thought comes to me, 'Do you think that this is the only earth that is in existence? Do you think that the human being is the only creative creature that is in manifestation now? You and your earth and your sun and moon are only a small portion of the great whole.' So you see, my friends, that we, even now, are in bondage with our thoughts because we cannot see the true significance of God's work. We think of it, selfishly, as only being towards the place we call 'Earth', but there are many earths and many galaxies that are beyond Man's comprehension. Who are we to say that God has not manifested his love in other places? I leave this thought with you because I feel that it will wet your appetite. It will set you thinking and help you to understand the true greatness of God in all aspects; that we are insignicant, just as the ants, in the comprehension of things; that we must evolve and grow until, perhaps, one day, our souls, if not our human thoughts will be able to accept, truly, the greatness of God's manifestations of love.

CHAPTER 8

Greater Realisation of Thought

As I again become conscious of what seems to be the beginning of another day, I realise how much progress I have made since I returned to spirit life. How much I have come to realise the power of thought.

Today, as I walk, I see my friend, Sloan. He is ahead of me. He seems to be sauntering along the road, kicking stones, very much as a schoolboy does and I am conscious of my friend who walks beside me. It seems at though we are going somewhere together. As we join up and walk along the road, there is no need for speech between us, we are in immediate attunement and we had picked up the thought from my friend that today we are being privileged to go in another direction. Before, we have always gone towards the realms that have not been quite so light as our own area of thought, but I am excited because I realise that I am going in a different direction towards more light and, I hope, more understanding of God's work.

As I walk, the air is beginning to have a rarified feel to it – as though each breath is like Spring – and my step becomes more eager as I go forward. I see ahead that there are two men and they beckon to us. I see that they are clothed quite differently from myself and my companions. It seems as though the clothes they wear are almost transparent and yet you cannot see through them. It is such a fine substance; there is such a pearl-like look to the material. I wish I could put it into words more adequately because I am sure there are people who would be very interested to find out the substance of the material that has been used in these garments. I realise that I am in the presence of ones who have gone on ahead of me in their soul development. These beings seem to be much lighter than myself. By lightness, I mean it is as though their aura picks up the light and it scintillates and glows around them. They smile at me because they realise that I am feeling quite inferior to them and I have the thought sent to me, 'We are all equal in God's eyes,' so no longer do I feel that I have no place here, but know that I would not be privileged to be here if there was not some divine purpose behind my visit.

As we walk up the slopes, we seem to be coming into what I would think was a mountain region. Yet, although we seem to be going higher, it does not get cold, as you would imagine. The scenery, to me, is very much like the land of Tibet. I see a monastery upon the mountain and I realise that this is where we are heading. It is as though we are, today, going forward to find out how other beings of light exist in their higher surroundings.

As I walk over what, on earth, would be considered a mountain pass, I feel no fear as regards my footing; I seem to be as sure-footed as a mountain goat, able to cope with the slopes and the stones underfoot. It seems as though something is lifting me up so that I do not stumble, and that I am protected and well-cared for.

I hear, in the distance, the tolling of a great bell. It is a wonderful sound - so rich and so deep - and it has a warmth with it - welcoming warmth, as if to say (almost like the sounding of the OM), 'Come! Come!', and I am more drawn towards the sound. My companions smile because they realise that I am sensitive enought to realise that this is the welcome that I am hearing. But it is not as a bell really, it is the thought that is sent out from the souls that are there that seems to be all-embracing and all-welcoming.

Now I am coming up a little path to what is a tiny gateway in a wall that seems so sheer, without any form, and there is a shadowy figure who opens the gate and beckons us inside. Although the gate is small, I do not have to bend my head. It seems as though the gate fits everyone who passes through, which is truly amazing, and it brings to thought the words in the Bible that Man must pass, as the camel, through the eye of the needle to be able to enter Heaven. I feel as though I am truly going further towards God's true meaning of Heaven. As I walk through the coolness of this place, I hear the chanting of ones who are in meditation. I feel a love and devotion here. I feel as though, just to be in the presence of these people, is almost like being bathed in love and understanding.

I see through the gloom that I am going towards a wonderful room and, in this room, it seems to be almost like archives. There are giant books; books that would take two men to lift because they are leather-bound and beautifully tooled and fashioned. I see two monks (as I would call them for want of a better name) lifting a book and laying it down lovingly and opening the pages to show me the beautiful painting that is there. The figuring around the letters is beautiful and the colours are out of this world (as we would say on the earth plane, because they are not of your world, they are truly perfection). Each letter is like looking at a stained-glass window and, as you look into the letters, you seem to see and feel a story behind the meaning of the picture that is with the letter. You begin to realise that you are not individually reading a story but you are feeling the love and devotion that has been placed in this book by loving hands which have fashioned this thing of extreme beauty for others, such as I, to come and read the passage of Man in time, the beauties of the soul and the beauty of God's universe and of his Heaven.

I begin to realise that Man is so insignificant. He is but a grain of sand upon the shore, and God's work is so great that it is ridiculous to think that it is only manifested towards human

Man. There must be other species of people in other places because it is so great (the work that is done) that it is impossible to think that this is all to be made manifest upon one small, insignificant earth.

I feel very fulfilled at the beauty I see and feel, and the ones who have opened the book smile at me and gradually turn the page. As the page turns, I see the thoughts of Man – the purity of mind that could be if Man would only be willing to let his thoughts be purified by the love of God and His understanding. As the page continues, so you see the passage of Man in time and how he has fallen by the wayside, such as in the parable of the sower when the seed fell upon stony ground and the weeds grew up and choked it and it died from lack of soil, water and love. As it goes on down the picture, I begin to realise that Man, in his evolution, has not always progressed, but digressed, and I feel suddenly sad when I realise how much beauty and love God makes manifest towards Man and how Man turns it into something ugly for his own use.

They sense that I am sad and they smile and turn another page. Here, I realise, is the beginning of what is normally called 'The Golden Age', and I see that, at last, Man is beginning to realise that he must live in unison with his fellow man. He must turn his cheek whenever a wrong is done to him so that he, in turn, can be forgiven for things that he does. I begin to realise that there is hope for Man yet to come, that this hope is born within us. It is as though we are programmed to find this light, this hope and this understanding. I see that there is, truly, someone who will come to take the mantle again – to go forward to bring light, a great light into the planet called 'Earth'. I realise that this time is not too distant, that it can come, that it is there in the plan of God's will, but it is waiting to see whether Man will be foolish enough to mar this and alter the pages of time and history so that this beauty will not come through and evolve.

I begin to realise that, whoever painted this book had great knowledge of life and a great understanding of God's love and will. They smile at me as much as to say, 'Another lesson you have learnt this day.' I hear a bell peeling, not too stridently, just gently upon the ear and I am beckoned forward because this is the time when they have their feast – or realease from fasting – and, although it is frugal food in human thought, to them it is wonderful. Although we have no need for food (I realised this some time ago), it is just the joining together, as was done in the time of Jesus – the breaking of bread and drinking of wine – just a small communion within ourselves; a recognition of God's renewal of life of Man and an understanding between us that we are all part of the same brotherhood, of the same family, of the same Father.

As I sit with these wonderful beings, I begin to realise that, in their cloistered life, they are reliving a life that they had upon the earth plane, where they were fully in meditation and thought towards their fellow man. These people gave unselfishly of themselves in the service of others. They thought not of their own needs but only to send thought and light into the darkest crevices of earth so that Man, himself, could bring forth light and understanding. I begin to realise that these people are ones who have fled from a land that has been overrun and religion is not thought of – a place where to be as they are, full of light and learning, would not be tolerated or understood. and I begin to realise the true significance of this building – this wonderful old citadel of hope and light. I realise that these people, by their thought patterns, have built again a replica of something that was with them when they were on the earth plane and that, through the wonders of spirit, they have been able to retrieve the treasures and the knowledge that were lost. By the power of thought, they have been able to reproduce the books and the understanding and the feeling of God's light and love. I realise how wonderful thought is, how Man misuses thought. I have seen thought in action. A careless thought, a hurtful thought can bring untold damage to a sensitive soul. I see that a kind thought can grow into something more beautiful. A love that builds with thought is a wonderful thing and I realise that Man will never truly evolve to the proper place that God would wish for him until he has learned to control his thoughts so that he would never think ill of another. His thoughts must always be used to bring light and love and understanding to all his fellow men.

As I think these things, so there seems to be a light that is building around me and it is almost a though the light is a revelation to me of this wonderful love that could be ours when we are on earth if only we had common sense and realised that we are truly children of God. There is no need for one to fight the other; there is no need for one to say, 'This is mine and you are not having it'; there is no need to hurt someone's feelings by being spiteful or thoughtless; and if Man, in his lifetime, could think of other people instead of himself, what a wonderful and beautiful life it could be upon the earth! Those who are hungry could be fed; those who are in need could be given help and those who had plenty would know the wonderful feeling of fulfillment when they saw that someone who was infirm and in need was helped. When they saw the face of a hungry child being fed; and when they saw that their thoughts and actions would have much to do with how the thoughts and actions of the future generations would be. So you see, there is so much to think of here; there is so much to find understanding about.

I feel my companions, Sloan and my friend who walks beside me, as though they are calling me and saying, 'Come, enough for this day! We have been privileged to be here, but our time is nearly over and we must return to our own sphere of life. We must try to go forward and to bring about the means for us to evolve towards their level of thought.' I begin to realise that I must truly take myself to task because there must be something that I have done, or have thought, or have willed that has placed me just slightly lower than these people. So I must try now to rid myself of bad thought; to think only of helping others and to try to find God's light and understanding. I think the most important thing in my spirit life now will be to try to help people upon the earth plane to think in a different way; to act in a different way and to show love to one another. Love that is beyond all jealousies and passions, love that passes all understanding so that it can truly add to the love that God sends towards Man, and make the world a far better place to live in.

I see, again, the green fields of home and I again hear the birds singing in the trees. For a moment, I feel nostalgic for my home, but it is only for a fleeting moment of time. I know that I am truly lucky to be where I am, that I am beginning to understand the true meaning of God's thought of Man, the true meaning of thought itself and to remember to be thoughtful of others. To remember that I am capable of all thought penetration; that I can send bad thought or good thought; that I must always be on the side of light. It would not do others on the earth plane harm to realise that they too should watch their thoughts because it is by their actions and thoughts at this moment of time that their time in spirit will be governed. It is time now for everyone who is alive on the earth plane to realise that they have inherited a wonderful gift of thought and that it should only be used for the benefit of Mankind. It should only be used to bring forward God's love and will upon the earth plane. I think that, when I truly can settle down to writing, I will base my book on thought – thoughts of love and understanding and great feeling for other people.

CHAPTER 9

The Pride of Place for Love

Since my transition, I have done many things. I have been patient because I was fully aware that all things must form a pattern and that I must conform to the pattern of life in my environment, but deep within me was the thought of love for my family and the comfort and the knowledge that they could be with me and near me. So, as I became fully aware of the day beginning, I waited eagerly for my friend to come so that I could be close to him and ask him, in my own way, 'When will I be able to join with my loved ones and feel their nearness to me again?'

His thought towards me, when he came, was quite sincere and he said, 'You must wait a little while longer and be patient because love is a thing that is hard to assess and here, in the spiritual realms, we do not necessarily meet everyone we knew in our last incarnation'. I thought to myself, 'This seems strange!' and, again, he speaks to me and says, 'No, it is not strange. You will find that there are people with whom you have been on a finer vibration, ones with whom you have been more spiritually in tune and, although there has been earthly love for these people, the spiritual love must also come to the foreground. You will understand fully later, when these reunions do come, that there is truth in my words.'

I felt strangely puzzled and apprehensive because I thought of my mother and my father. I thought of my childhood and of my need for them in the past and the need they had for me before they passed over into spirit life, and I wondered if that love I felt then was truly of a spiritual nature as well as of a physical nature. So I was quite disquieted for a while because I thought to myself, 'Well, here I am, and I thought that everyone would meet and we would all join and be happy together,' and now I have to realise that, although perhaps I was compatible with people on earth, I am not quite so compatible in my spiritual acceptance of their life here. It seems strange to me. I am afraid that I must think about this for quite a while before I will be able to absorb these thoughts because it is a strange way of reasoning and thinking. But he smiles at me, as much as to say, 'You may be a little apprehensive now, but later on, when the time is ready for you to make these close relationships again, you will realise quite fully the true meaning of what I am saying.' So I think to myself, 'Well, he has been very fair and kind and understanding towards me in everything that has happened to me since I have been here, and I must place trust in this guide. After all, that is what he truly is to me – a guide, a helping hand, someone who knows my thoughts, who leads me ever onwards towards knowledge.

So I try to place these thoughts aside – to shelve them for a moment of time – so that I do not feel sad in any way for not being able to make contact immediately with my loved ones. But I realise there is more in heaven and earth than we mere mortals think of. We seem to think that everything revolves around us and that everything is ours by right, but here I am beginning to realise that you must earn these rights. It is a love that is given from a wise Father – one who realises that there must be much thought and much justice in and around the work that is done here. People must be able to understand fully the true working out of our lives through our spirit life so that everything is accomplished in the right way and in the right manner.

Again, he smiles at me and he beckons and I shrug my

shoulders and think to myself, 'Well, I will think of it another day.' Perhaps that day will not be too far away. I must go forward now to see what more is to be offered to me in the way of knowledge. As I go towards him, he pats my shoulder with his hand as much as to say, 'Be of good cheer! We are friends, are we not?' and I smile back at him because I realise that, without him, I feel as though I am alone and I do not want to be alone here. I want to be able to understand fully the true meaning of God's Heaven. We, on earth, have a different concept of the Heavenly realms. We only think of choirs and angels. We do not realise that there is much here that will seem mundane, even to the most spiritual of us because, as we go on being taught we have to go through every aspect of earthly life and spiritual life until we are able to place them together so that they are bonded completely and we are, at last, at one with ourselves.

How many people, upon the earth plane, seem to take pride in themselves and feel as though they are wonderful and capable and the only ones who have such marvellous thoughts and yet this place is a great leveller of people. You are all equal. No-one is better than anyone else and you must treat other people in a civilised and proper manner. You must never think bad thoughts and yet, on the earth plane, we seem to sail merrily through life, stepping on one person and then stepping on another. We do not worry if we take away their pride in everything that they do. We do not worry if we take away the love that they try to give to others – that we destroy it and turn it into bitterness.

Here, it is a true opening of one's eyes. Truly, one sees right through everything that has gone on in earth existence. Everything that has gone before is analysed, scrutinised and put in it's own place ready for someone to come along later and assess it. I assess myself, as I assess others that are around me – not in a cruel manner, but in a way that sees perhaps they are better than I and that I am insignificant to them. Still, they always show love towards me, and understanding, such as my guide and friend. He always shows love and understanding towards me and I take pride in this love because I realise that to be able to love someone whom you know is inferior to yourself is a great lesson in life. To begin to realise that that person is no less than yourself and is, perhaps, in some ways, a greater being.

On earth you can never measure the spirituality of one man against the other because it does not show through. Only those who are lucky enough to be clairvoyant are able to see the true inner selves of the people whom they meet. I wish that I had been able to have this gift before I left earth because I think that many times I made very bad judgements in assessing other people. Many times I have judged people wrongly and have learnt to my cost, so I say that you must never judge one another. You must always assess the person fairly – their likes and dislikes, their mannerisms, their ways, the way they treat other people. Really, the way they treat other people is more important than anything else. Upon the earth, we tend to think only of material conditions and material surroundings and the assets that people have. We do not count the assets of a kindly heart and a pure soul; we count how much money they have in the bank, whether or not they are good for lending money, whether or not we can use them in some way to further our own plans. Here, there is nothing to gain. You only have to assess one another to make sure that you really understand the other person and know the true quality that is within them.

My friend beckons to me and he is showing me a pathway which is rugged and a little off the beaten track. As I walk along, I am aware of salt being gathered and I think, 'Why should salt be gathered here?'. I then realise that the sea I am looking at must have salt in it as otherwise things would not be so buoyant as they are. Everything seems to be popping like corks on water – up and down, up and down! I see boats so clearly. I see people laughing and enjoying themselves. I look at my friend and he says, 'Yes, it is the power of thought and the love that is between them – the bond of love – that draws these people together so they can be happy and content in whatever environment they find themselves. Today, they are enjoying themselves in the water and on the water, and they are happy and content. Tommorrow, they may be in quite a different environment altogether and they may be with a different band of people – ones who are more fitting to that day's thought.' Then I begin to realise that it is thought that powers everything. That perhaps I, later on, may be able to channel my thoughts so that I may be able to link up sometimes with one group of friends or relatives, sometimes with another, and I begin to take hope by this and I think to myself, 'I am learning! Perhaps this is what I am lacking – the understanding of the true feeling of love.'

I wonder how many people, when they were on the earth plane, have sworn that their romance was the greatest love of their life and yet, in many cases, it turned out to be a dead and infertile thing and so, probably, was only infatuation. I realise that it is only here that you can really tell the true measure of love and understanding, and I look forward to this. My friend smiles and says to me, 'Again, you have learnt another lesson of life – a lesson that we cannot always expect to have what we want. We cannot always expect everyone to conform to a pattern. We cannot always expect ones we want to be near us to be near us because we have to earn the right to have the privilege of their love and understanding.'

Suddenly, I begin to realise that there is truly much to be learnt here, much to find and much to do and I am content again. I feel again the longing for my family and I realise that I must go forth to share my thoughts with others before I can ask selfishly for something for myself.

CHAPTER 10

The University of Spirit

I again awake refreshed, and full of hope and joy because I have been told that I shall go into the halls of learning to see how the running of spirit life begins. To see how the ones who would wish to be used place themselves forward to gain much knowledge and light and understanding so that they can, in turn, be of assistance to those upon the earth plane who, with like mind, would wish to serve their Father, God.

I feel quite apprehensive as I enter the portals of this building because I know, in the future, if I can establish myself and bring forward the right feeling and the right thought, that I, too, will be able to be used in such a manner. I do not wish to be a guide or a great teacher, but I wish to be able to be used to bring forth knowledge from the spirit world towards the earth so that the ones who are left behind me can benefit from the light that I have seen.

As I go into this wonderful building, I see eager faces and the light that is about them. I realise that some of these souls have really worked hard to bring themselves to this position where they can be taught to be used for the furtherance of God's will. I see that there is only eagerness with them, there is no tiredness or disillusionment. They are completely absorbed in what their tutors are saying to them and the words of knowledge that are being imparted towards them. There are all different aspects of mediumship being talked of. They are being shown the elemental stages of mediumship. They are being shown the rudest forms of communication such as table-rapping, the moving of tables and articles and the knockings upon walls and things of this nature, such as we, ourselves have heard of and have, perhaps, witnessed in our own search towards spirit communication. Then they progress forward to see the different aspects of mediumship. Physical mediumship (which can bring materialisation of spirit), direct voice and clairvoyance – and they see how mind pictures are transferred to the mediums for interpretation. They also see how mediums can sit in circles perhaps for years before they start to develop and sometimes, during their course of communication and help, they are taken by the guides into circles, and they see how the vibrations are blended and how different ones come forward to perform different workings towards the furtherance of development. Then they are shown how the voice box is built up out of ectoplasm when direct voice is used, and how the substance that is used is so different from the ectoplasm that is used when a spirit fully materialises in front of an audience during a seance.

I, myself, am beginning to understand fully how much work goes on from the spirit realms to bring about these forces that can be used upon the earth plane. I, too, have been privileged to go to a circle and to see the emanations that are coming from the ones who sit. You can see the ones who will become healers because of the colour rays that flow through them. Then you see the medium who will be used for trance and the one who will be used for clairvoyance. Then you see the one who will become more of an orator. You see the ones who are ultra-sensitive and the ones who are just beginning to be sensitive. You see how spirit can approach them and draw near them without causing them concern or worry. You also see the ones who are foolish; who will play with games and try to draw spirit towards them, not caring whether it is good or bad. We have sat and watched these people in their desperate attempts to draw from spirit to prove that they, themselves, are knowledgeable and yet, my friends, they do not realise how much they are playng with fire. We see who is gathered in the room beside them and there is much darkness. There is very little light, and we realise that, if these people are not careful, they will draw to themselves something that they cannot control.

It is a very abject lesson when you look from the spirit side of life, because you know the full scope of spirit activity that can be drawn into such a room. Then you see a properly-run circle. You see the ones who are the protectors of the circle forming light shields that keep away the dark things which are around so that only light can penetrate into the circle to being forth knowledge. That is the proper way, and the proper means of developing a medium. Too much is said of the medium in regard to the standard of work. Very little is said of the teacher who fails to teach properly and it is a great thing that those who are now interested in the spiritualist way of life are advocating that these circles should be supervised and run in a proper manner. We see such foolishness with some people – what they see as spirit communication is only a self-hypnosis.

It is so revealing to be able to see, as from a distance, these people as they perform. I say 'perform' because it is a performance that is given, and we feel so sad that they have shut their minds off and accepted the lowest form of communication, and left the spirituality behind. They have not sought higher things but have been content, so, in their contentment, they will stay in that area of thought. They will never be able to develop themselves beyond it because their minds have closed. You have heard of people who would dearly love to go further with their work but, always, there is a mental block in front of them. This is a mental block that they put up themselves when they start to shut down their minds. Then you hear of the consequences of these mental blocks – you see people who have upset nervous systems. It is all because their minds have closed and yet, spiritually, the soul is pulling in another direction and so you get this imbalance in their lives and they are, as you say, not complete and not at peace.

Also , we see the healing factor. We see the beautiful rays that come from those who would wish to be healers. You can see the beauty in their souls because they, in their way, would rather give of themselves than receive and, to me, although there is much in mediumship, I would say that healing is the most useful gift. To those who would aspire to be mediums I would say: if you are given the gift of healing as well, then you are truly fortunate, because with this you have the purity of thought and light, and a generosity of mind and personality so that the person wishes, not for themselves, but for others to benefit. I know that you will find there are some who would wish to make material gains but it is not for us to judge, it is for us to understand that, sometimes, people's circumstances force them to do things that they would not normally do, so they must, in their need, help themselves as well as helping others, and who are we to decry them for that action.

Also, you see the ones who have developed to a certain stage and feel that they have nothing else that spirit or anyone upon the earth plane can teach them because they, themselves, are fully developed. You feel sorry for them because, in their smallness of mind, they have passed by what is beautiful and accepted only what they can carry in their hands. They will wonder, later on, why the gift seems to fade and no longer seems to be as much a fulfilment as it was.

Then you see the ones who are dedicated in mind – who do not worry over what happens to them in life, as long as they can be of service to God and to their fellow man; as long as they can bring forth truth and light. That is all-important – not the pettiness of human thought, but a universal thought that goes out, grasping the whole world in its concept and embracing all men as brothers. Seeing, not the colour of one's skin or the religious understanding, but to know, within, that this, truly, is a soul that is in need of help and it is a child of God who is the soul; and no matter what persecution or detriment it brings to their lives, they will dedicate themselves to bringing about a fullness of God's love to be made manifest upon the earth.

These, truly, are the ones who will go far. It may not show upon the surface – people may think of them as just another medium – but the development that has gone on in the background is far superior to those who would think that they are the be-all and end-all. They, in their simplicity of mind, have been able to be moulded, as the clay by the sculpture, into a beautiful thing and, as they develop, so the beauty is made more manifest. You have seen the statue of David - the manifestation of thought from Michaelangelo. You have seen how wonderfully he has displayed the hands and all that is there; the beautiful feel of the statue and the aliveness of it, and you realise that here is a living thought. So these people who give themselves completely to God to be moulded and used in every aspect of life, in every aspect of giving and loving, truly bring forth beauty such as the statue. Beauty that is there for those who can discern to see and yet, on the surface of their lives, they have done little. But, my friend, it is not what is on the surface that shows that is important, it is what is within the soul.

People are foolish! They seem to think that what they can see is all-important, but I say to you that, if all of you could see yourselves as you truly are, you would be very surprised. You would realise that there is such a lot in you that needs helping and replenishing and refurbishing . It is very difficult to find the words to explain but, within the soul, people do not realise how much the imperfections show when you look at it from the spiritual side as I have been while sitting here in this teaching group, finding understanding of the light that works through the earth.

I am, at last, beginning to grasp and understand the true aspect of spirit communication. It is such a delicate thing. The vibrations are so important. We have heard people say at meetings or at services, 'Let us sing to raise our vibrations!', but it is not your vibrations, my friend, that need to be lifted – it is your thoughts and the purity of thought that need to be lifted. It is only that that can bring the higher communication. So, when you go to be with God and with your friends for a short while, leave behind the bias and the spitefulness of life and take a purity of thought with you so that everyone with whom you come into contact that day will feel as though something wonderful has touched their lives. As though they have found the true spirituality in life. Everything will seem to be in a different light and thus, as they go through their family life, through the week ahead, they will realise the benefit that they have found by the visit they have made to be together with God and their friends.

God sends his power and his love and his understanding, and the ones from the higher realms of spirit bring that love towards Man. But how many times does Man turn aside from that love and how many times does ego come forward to push aside the thoughts of others, to utilise everything so that there has to be something behind every action that is done - something that is material instead of spiritual? When you are on the material plane, we know it is very difficult to think on a spiritual level, and in spirit life it is very difficult to think on a material level. So I think, for quite a long time to come, there will always be this little gap between the ones on earth and the ones in spirit. We know that those who are called 'mediums' can be the ladder between the two, the ones who can lift the thoughts and lift those in spirit so that they can make communication. It is a funny way of putting things, I know, to say, 'lift those in spirit', but, unless they are helped by the medium and by the ones who work with the medium and through the medium, then, my friends, there would be no communication whatsoever because we, in the spirit life, have to wait, have to be shown, have to be directed and helped to be able to make communication with those upon earth. It is the love bond that is between us that draws us, that makes us want to understand how they are feeling; how they are coping with life. We, as we come into the full realisation of our passing, remember the ones who are left behind, and the love pattern that is built throughout our earthly lives towards one another is hard to break – a mother's love for her child, a father's love for his son or daughter. It is a very difficult situation when one passes into spirit, for we see the sadness that is with the ones left behind. Many do not seem to rest until they can communicate and let the ones on the earth plane know that they still exist; that they are still with them in thought and that there are means of communication.

But this is another aspect of mediumship which I would like to discuss later because it entails much from the medium to bring these communications. It is a thing that would need me to go into detail of greater length than I am prepared to do at this moment of time. So I will say to you: bear with me , my friends, and let me go on to the other aspects of work here.

CHAPTER 11

Man's Perseverance in the Face of Difficulties

As I again become conscious of my surroundings, I begin to realise that there has been much progress for me in the short time that I seem to have been in this wonderful place. I realise how Man struggles upon the earth plane with little knowledge or thought of spiritual matters; how life becomes materialistic and void of the contact with God and, as I look back on my own life, I see how lucky I have been. God has been there with me, helping me and, by his holy laws, guiding me. Although at first I was not aware of this because it is a subtle touch that you feel, yet, as your life grows and you become stronger and able to cope with things – as you start to reach maturity – then you fully realise how wonderful the contact of the love of God can be.

I wish that you could fully understand and realise the full potential of Man. We, in our ignorance, when we are in earth life, never use the gifts of God in the manner that they should be used. We treat everything as though it is of ourselves. If someone is gifted with singing or music, it is their own gift – it is how their throat was formed at the time of their birth that has made it slightly different from somone else so their voice is different! They do not see the implications of the gift coming from God and, if someone is born who seems to be quite endowed with brains and is able to count and write in a goodly manner, then this is considered also to be something that just happened – something without purpose which that person was lucky enough to have. They do not see the true meaning of

God's love made manifest. That he, in his wisdom, has given these gifts so that Man can benefit - not only for himself, but for other people as well, so that although they are not so well endowed with gifts, they can listen to someone who has a beautiful voice; they can hear someone who is able to make an instrument, as you would say, 'talk'; and they are able to use the brain of the mathematician so that things can be calculated and the ignorant helped to count and to write.

You see in some people a great dedication towards their fellow Man – the ones who decide to become teachers because they feel that they want to help the children of the poor who are being left behind in evolution of Man. Children who are not realising their full potential of learning because of the cost of teaching, the running of the schools and the administration.

Then you find the dedicated nurses and doctors who will toil long hours for poor pay; who do it because they love mankind and wish to help everyone who is in need. There are many who struggle diligently in poorly paid material employment to support their families and to keep their sense of pride that they are able to do so .

Then there are the ones who are unemployed through no fault of their own. Those who seem to be losers in life – those who, perhaps, are unemployable because of their lack of education in the past. It is these people who need help because they struggle so hard to fight against the tide of materialism. They cannot swim as strongly as the others and so they are left behind on their own level of thought. But, my friends, as things are to be, there will be many who will be placed in this category who are not uneducated. It will be the fault of times to comes, when people will have to learn to spend their time wisely. If they have idle hands, then they must help the community; they must think of others. join in schemes for the necessary building and work to be done so that others can benefit.

You see, Man is constantly in a struggle – if it is not a physical struggle, it is a mental struggle – because life is beginning to move so fast that Man cannot keep up with it

Man seems not to be able to cope, except on his own level, and there are so many levels of thought that there can be no generalisation of this. It is entirely up to the individual how things affect them and how they manage to overcome them. So it is in spirit life, because many people still seem to bring with them their material thoughts of the struggle they have had upon the earth plane, and it takes quite a time for them to be able to lay this aside and to realise that there is no need to struggle. That thought and love are the two essential things here; that each one of us, although we may be on different levels of thought, are equal with each other; and it is a wonderful power of thought within you; that education does not count here; that one of us, although we may be on different levels of thought, are equal with each other; and it is a wonderful experience to realise how a soul has evolved.

When I was on the earth plane, I always treated my friend, Sloan, with respect because I knew that his circumstances and his education were not as good as mine. Now I am here in spirit life, I realise that it is he who is more advanced in spirit life than myself. I was lucky to have advancement on the earth and I did not realise the full potential that was with my friend. It is only since I have been in spirit life that I realise that, when I was polishing up on my arithmetic, reading and writing, he was working and learning about life and the right way to live his life. Through his dedication to his work for his Father, God, he was replenishing himself spiritually, not materially as I was at that time, and I realise now that, if ever I have a chance to be used in any way, I would be only too glad to sacrifice any material condition so that I could advance on a spiritual level.

As I speak to you, my friends or children (because I feel that you are children that I am speaking to - children of the same Father, the same power, that I was); you, in your earth life, now have a chance to realise that there is so much more to life than I was aware of and it is my endeavour to bring forward this light and knowledge towards you so that you do not waste time on the trivialities of materialistic life. You should be able to open yourself up to all the power that is around you and the love that comes with this power so that you will truly find an advancement in your soul's growth and not in material conditions.

We do not mean that you should not have a nice home, a nice family and, perhaps, a car or things that you feel are an asset to your family life, but we do say to you that, hand-in-hand with the growth of your material considerations, you should always start to consider: How much have I progressed in this life that I have been given? How well am I shaping up for the life that will come when it is time for me to leave this place?

I say to you that the time that you spend upon the earth plane is such a short span of time, and Man is very prone to wasting time. He fills it with unnecessary things – anything to pass the time away. He does not realise, until it is too late, that time wasted is never returned to you; that it is only the time that you give to others, that is returned to you and added to your span upon the earth plane. There are many people who walk the earth who do not realise that they are, as you would say, 'living on borrowed time'. There are many people who for the want of prayer, would have passed into spirit life. They do not realise that someone, somewhere, has sent prayer out for healing or help for them in a situation that they find unbearable. You see, time is a very precious thing – waste nothing of it, my friends, lest you should reach my side of life and look back with regret.

Although I, myself, thought that I was doing everything that was right in regard to my search for spiritual unfoldment, I can see now the pitfalls and the time-wasting by I did by chasing outlandish theories which, when they were tested, did not hold together. Too many times, scientists sit and test others to see if they can find a flaw in the power and the love that is manifesting, perhaps in a medium, or even in one who can use their mind to be trained to move objects. They will test them and test them and write their findings in books and references and yet the next person who comes along does not believe what they have written or tested and have it tested again. No-one accepts anything as fact and yet, in our orthodox religions, we are expected to take everthing on face value as regards Heaven and the Christed ones who have come to show light upon the earth. We are asked to accept, blindly, that eternal life is there for us and yet, when proof is given, it is ignored and set aside.

So, I think that Man will struggle for a great many years before the truth will finally sink in that religion is not a need for dogma or creed. That it is a way of thought, a way of activating thought so that people can benefit by this thought; a way of making love work in the way God wished it to, that it should pass from one to another as if it were forming links in a chain. Not a chain to be around your neck, one that would be a heavy burden, but a fine, gold thread of light that joins one soul to another so that love and understanding can be built between people. People not only of one nation, but all people. There should be no difference in thought between ones who have had education and the native in the jungle. Sometimes, Man has not evolved as much as he thinks. Sometimes, the native has found another way that is easier to link with this God-force and it is the one who thinks he is educated, and that the native is ignorant, who is losing out in the race of time to find God.

Now I sit here in meditative thought, thinking of Man and how, perhaps, one day, he will progress so far that the struggle will be taken out of life and that everyone who is born will feel as though they are in, what is loosely termed, 'a golden age' where Man will love his brother; and sacrifice his own feelings so that the feelings of his brother may not be disturbed. One man will share with another when there is not much to eat and when there is plenty. We take for granted the gifts of God – the rain, the sun and the earth – because these things are necessary in our lives so that we can eat and be able to regenerate and to continue upon the earth plane.

But, be not wrapped up too much in material thoughts of food for the stomach and the body. It is food for the soul that is the most important factor of all. Man, in his ignorance, often passes this by.

CHAPTER 12

My Endeavour to Learn not to Appease

How many times, in earth life, do people seek to find a way of appeasement so that they, in their endeavour, may not lose face but be able to change circumstances in their own favour by giving another something to keep them, as you would say, 'quiet' on their behalf? You would be surprised how many people come into spirit life still thinking that, in some way, they can change things so that they can be accepted. They little realise the true significance of God's knowledge of them and that everything that is done during a life circle is tabulated and checked, down to the finest detail.

We often think, when we are in earth life, that what other people cannot see they will never find out about. This is where Man makes his mistake because he little realises how truly his Father knows him, how truly he is understood and loved – even for his faults and his transgressions. I, myself, when I came into spirit life, was quite unaware of how or what my life here would be, then I realised that I must be true to myself and true to the one whom they call 'God' so that I, in my own way, would not seek to change things to suit myself. We know, when we are here, that we are able to use our thought pattern much more strongly than we ever thought possible, but this thought pattern must be directed towards good or it seems to make no progress. Man will soon realise that it is only by opening himself towards God that full progress can be made.

Today, my friend, Sloan has beckoned me because I am to go on a journey – a journey through the planes of thought towards the earth. I am fortunate because, today, I will be able to see the one who I will use in the future – one who will help me with my work when I try to put mental thought to paper for ones, such as you who are opening this book, to read.

I find I am going into a very peaceful atmosphere. I see the ones who protect the circle standing around and enfolding them in a cocoon of love. I see the one who is to be the one I shall use and I see that she is in, what would be called, the 'early stages of development'. I look at Sloan and he realises my thoughts are 'Will this person ever be able to be controlled by me so that I may be able to bring forth these truths?' He smiles and says, 'You will be able to watch her progress and you will be surprised because, behind that facade is a quiet mind and an open heart, and this is all that is required.'

I listen and see the ones who are in the role of teachers draw close to the child, because the ones from spirit are very close to her. I see her auric field and I see the penetration of spirit light into that auric field and I begin to realise that, at least, someone is penetrating enough to make themselves felt upon her. I realise that this is a wonderful process – how things can materialise in such a way that one, such as she, can be used in such a capacity. I listen, with interest, to the divination of how the meanings of the symbols that are given to these people by spirit are interpreted. I am aware that there us a great feeling of love and a wonderful light – a blue light – that seems to be around everyone who sits. I see a chain of gold passing between them, as though they, themselves, were links in the chain, and I realise that these people are in perfect attunement with one another. The 'vibrations', as you would say, are truly matched and I can feel the harmony and the love that is between them. I see not the earthly bodies but the souls and the growth of the souls that are there, and I realise how much people lose upon the earth plane by not being able to understand fully the true meaning of spirit; because we are all spririt, although we do not realise it whilst we are still walking around and acting foolishly in a human form.

I look at Sloan and send thought of him: 'How long will it take?', and he says, 'In earthly time, quite some time; but in our time, not too long to make you impatient. We will come back now and again to see how things are formulating and what progression is being made'. I withdrew from the room feeling much happier than when I arrived, knowing that at least, now, things were beginning to form, ready for me to be able to come and speak thus so that it can be written on paper, so that people can read and understand my thoughts.

I am glad that I am being privileged enough to be able to be used in this way. To be able to understand again and to be able to try to rectify some of the thoughts I had which were not truly in attunement with the truth. Do not think, when I make this statement, that I am saying that I have declared falsehoods in my writing – I do not mean this, but I mean that, at last, I am beginning to realise the full extent of truth. I am beginning to understand more fully the love of God and the work that the ones from spirit do to try to help those who come in need. I, myself, was very pleased, when sitting in a seance room, to hear members of my family coming and talking to me. I feel I was very priviledged to have been able to experience these things and now I feel doubly priviledged to be able to go forward and to be able to be used to help to bring light towards you in the earth plane.

Do not worry, my friends. There is still time for you to be able to change your ways and think more of your brothers and sisters upon the earth plane. To be able to lay aside thought of appeasement, to be able to stand sqaurely and look at yourselves and to see your own thoughts and put them right. I come with a warning to you – to watch and mend your ways while there is still time for you upon the earth plane because you are the ones who are your own judge and your own jury.

You, yourselves, are the ones who must assess. You, your-selves, must be the ones who realise how much you have done in your lives that is not as God would wish.

Do not worry so much over earthly rules – think of the laws of God. These laws were made with love towards you. With-out the laws of God, there would be no earth, no seasons, no growth of corn or growth of animals. There would be no growth of the human race. There would be no knowledge or understanding. Things would become a void. Nothing would grow. Everything would become barren and you, yourselves, would perish and would disappear from the planet called 'earth'. In fact, everything would, as you would say, 'die' and be gone forever. It is only God's love and His understanding that keep the freshness of the green grass, the blue of the sky, the sunshine that keeps you warm and the love of your parents and families.

So listen, my children. Think of my words. Do not wait until you come into spirit life, to try to put things right. You have the chance now – take it with both hands! It is very important, more important than you could ever realise because it is your future that you are thinking of – not your future here upon the earth plane, but your future in spirit life, where it is more important for you to make progress. As you make your progress, you will understand more fully the meaning of my words because your lives will take on more meaning. You will find more joy in the things you do because you will not be sending out spiteful thoughts. You will think of other people and their feelings. You will think of other lands and their needs, and you will always find that there is someone else who is in greater need than yourselves. So I say to you: 'Think! Think! Think!'

CHAPTER 13

The Return of Thought

I know, when you see the heading for this chapter, you will wonder what 'return of thought' means, but I say to you that those upon the earth plane who do not marshal their thoughts into channels of goodness, do not realise that thought sent out with malice and bitterness often returns to the sender. They do not realise, in their lives, why things do not seem to go right with them. They cannot understand why someone should suddenly act in a strange manner towards them and reject them or subject them to feelings that they are not wanted, or not cared for. Sometimes these feelings of rejection are really the return of thought that they have sent out in their lives to others.

Thought is the most powerful thing and people do not realise the full potential of the human brain. They do not realise that everything that is thought or done in a life is recorded. You know when an aeroplane has a serious accident (or 'crash' as you call it), they immediately send someone to look for the little black box which holds the recording of conversations and actions of the pilot, co-pilot and the crew. It is so with yourselves – there is a part of your mind that records all these things and they are stored in what we call the 'subconscious' for lack of further knowledge of what it is, or what it consists of.

There are many learned men upon the earth plane who

categorise the brain as the most wonderful computer of all. But I say to you it is only a computer – only what is fed into it can be used. When we are children, we learn our tables and our lessons at school and this knowledge, although we think we forget, is transferred by the brain into the part which we call the subconscious and it seems to stay there, never to return. But I say to you, my children, that this is a fallacy because every thought that you think is recorded. You might say: it would take too many tapes on a computer to hold such recordings of a lifetime, and yet I say to you: your brain has the capacity to carry all this knowledge, stored, without ever overloading the computer.

When you come to think of this, you realise the true wonder of God's creations. In animals, birds and insects, you see this force of life – where a cow, who is young (or any animal), knows instinctively what is needed; even to the smallest cat or dog, they know exactly what to do when they give birth to their young. Instinctively, they know! Also, with pigeons and birds, they know exactly what to do, how to return to their home. The birds that migrate to foreign countries know instinctively where they must go and how they will return. Even the fish know insinctively when the time comes for them to spawn and to bring forth their young, even if their passage home is so difficult that, like the salmon, they die in thousands after they have spawned and brought forth the new progeny. You see, my friends, their minds, although small, are able to store knowledge enough for their needs, and I say to you that Man has greater storage capacity than is ever used or needed at this moment of evolution but, as Man evolves into the future, greater knowledge of the human brain and mind will come forth and they will be able to understand the full potential of God's wonderful gift of life.

You, in your ignorance, the same as I, never realise how much the wonders of God are about us and what creative force brings forth the smallest flower, the smallest bird and the minutest insect that walks upon the earth plane. We like to delve back into history and think of prehistoric Man and all the animals that have gone before. All these seemed so large in the past, as we are able to conjure up by the finding of bones and fossils – yet we do not realise that this is only one cycle of Man; that it is a continuous cycle, that it is not only once that these creatures have been upon the earth. That it is not only once that there were men such as the stone-age men and that, every time this cycle comes and goes, the earth survives and Man disappears, only to be regenerated into another form of Man.

As we think of the 'evolvement' of Man, we think of the stages of evolution from one-celled creatures onwards. We see how things are formulated in the minds of the biologists and scientists and sometimes, in the spirit world, we could laugh at the ignorance of these people in the way they treat the communication from one world to another. We see how mediums and people who have psychic ability are tested time and time again, and then the scientists do not believe the truths of another scientist and so they will test again, covering the same ground with such a futile waste of time. They cannot accept anything unless they see it in black-and-white. They do not realise that there is a greater intervention which can change black-and-white into grey, and bring it back into black-and-white again for a full realisation of truth. You must feel sorry for these people because, in their lack of understanding of God and the principles of nature and of life, they, in their ignorance, are only scratching the surface. They are not able to see farther than the noses upon their faces. They do not realise that, by opening their minds, they can gain great knowledge and great understanding.

You my children, who are reading this book, I ask you to think well upon my words. It is with simplicity of mind, and truth, I bring forward my life from the spirit to you so that you, yourselves, will understand fully what is in your future. Be not afraid of the passage of time. You are going towards something far more beautiful than you realise. Man is afraid to speak of death. It is a word, now, that is not used. It is something that people would prefer not to mention because it is not thought to be the best subject to be talking about, yet I say to you that, in the midst of life, we are with death and we do not fully understand the way that this transition is made. It is just as much a traumatic thing to be born as it is to pass into spirit. In fact, it is harder for the soul that is being brought down to your level to start again upon the earth plane than for the one that is being released from the heaviness of an aged body to find an exuberance of life here in this plane of thought. So I say to you, children of earth: be not afraid when it is your time to come forward. Think not, dwell not, on these things; just think of it as a new day dawning, a new door that is opening before you, with so much for you to be able to grasp and to learn; with so much for you to be able to do; with so much for you to be able to do for others, because, in helping others, you truly help your own progression.

I have learnt much since I have been here, I know, at first, it was hard for me to realise that, immediately, I could not be where I would wish to be (with the ones I love), but now I have become accustomed to the thought that soon, when the time is ready, I shall be able to meet with them. I say to you that when you pass into spirit life, it is only a matter of time before everything is placed into perspective and then you are able to go forward in light and love.

Do not expect to be given a harp, wings or a halo. You are as you are – a child of God. He knows exactly who you are and what you are, through and through. He sees you with the love of a father and yet is not of human form. He is the life-giving force of love and He is the ultimate of everything.

CHAPTER 14

The Cornerstone of Life

I am fully aware of my shortcomings and realise that, when I was upon the earth, there was much I thought I knew which, in this life, will have to be, as you would say, 'unlearnt' and re-lived again. Even if it cannot be done from a human set of rules, I must endeavour, in my spiritual thoughts, to put things into motion so that my thoughts can be placed in a better frame of mind. I look forward very much to the work that is ahead. I realise that there will be much consideration of hit-and-miss. I realise that there are many factors to be taken into account, such as my own spiritual wish to help the people of earth, and my contact with the one I will use as, for want of a better word, I call my'medium'.

In her development, I have stood shoulder to shoulder with those who have endeavoured to bring about the wonderful progress of the training, with the devotion that goes into that 'training' of a medium. I have stood and watched the tedious workings from spirit which, to Man, would seem to take so long and yet is done to such a state of perfection that nothing is allowed to be left to chance. I began to realise, then, how much there is in heaven and earth; how much is the co-operation of life from one side to the other; how wonderful is the thought of being able to bridge the gap between two worlds. To be able to step, for a moment, from one dimension to another, in time that takes no longer than the batting of an eye-lid, where it is so swift and so true.

I am filled with anticipation as to what my work will entail. How I can bring forward, through this person who is so willing to lend herself, spiritual influence to make an impact on her so as to make it possible for me to bring forth my work. I have seen how much it entails – how much love is given from one sitter to another, how the bond grows between them and how the colours blend, and the vibrations.

If you could see yourselves each moment of the day, you would realise fully what beautiful colour vibrations come with your thoughts; even if they are not good thoughts, the colours are in profusion. I, myself, wish now to bring about muted colours of love so that what I may be able to transmit through this person will bring the love that is here from God towards Man. The love that is here from those you would say are the angelic hosts – the ones who are the guides, the helpers and the teachers who come steadfastly to bring light towards the earth people.

Then, further up the chain there comes the reality of those who have come before, many times. Those who have been Christed, who have been fully evolved so they are gone beyond my realm of light – gone further towards the God-head – so that only the radiance of them is left, as an essence, to permeate the very air that we exist in. The light that comes from God, and the strength, the feeling of energy that is always present is as when you walk upon a mountain and you breathe the rarified air and you begin to realise how high the mountain is and how much nearer to God's Heaven it seems. But, of course, Man's concept of Heaven is often wrong. He does not realise that Heaven and earth mingle – that one overlaps the other, and that we are all in existence in the same world, even though it is as two worlds. And who am I to judge whether there is another world entwined with ours. This is not permitted for me to see, but I feel as though, one day, there may be further revelations for me to be able to find, and to expound towards you upon the earth plane. I feel that this is for the future and not for the present. At this moment of time, I am busy trying to bring forward what is necessary for me to give to the one who will be used by me so that she, in her way, can put my pen to paper.

As I am thinking these thoughts, again Sloan is with me and he brings my friend who travels with me. They join me in thought about the process of work that is ahead. Sloan nods to me and beckons, and I know that it is time for me to walk with him to find more light, more truth and, as I go upon my way, I feel apprehensive because I feel as though something important is ahead – just as when you are a child, you feel an excitment within yourself, as though something is building up to a surprise. The surprise comes, because I see, coming down the path to meet me, the one with whom I have shared my earth life. Her smile is radiant towards me, and my step quickens because I know that, at last, this is the joy that I have wished for and longed for – to again feel the touch of her hand and the kiss upon my cheek. I am pleased! I am happy and content because I know now that my path ahead will not be a lonely path, that there will be times of contact and that we will be able to spend many Heavenly hours together, as, when we were on the earth plane, we spent earthly hours together. My mind again returns to my home and she smiles, as much as to say, 'Look back not into the past, but to our future together – the future that we can make for ourselves, the future we can use to help others.'

I am content and, as I am in this state of contentment, suddenly she seems to have faded from my line of vision again, but I am not sad because I know, truly, that we shall be together whenever it is necessary for us to be together. That very thought gives me strength to be able to continue to do what I must do. The work that I have chosen to begin must now start because I feel that, at last, by being able to be in contact with her, I have been given what may be termed on earth, the 'go-ahead' to be able to start my work, to revise my thoughts and put pen to paper.

CHAPTER 15

Contact

Now, I am able, by thought process, to move around more actively. To be able to, as you would say, 'visit' many places; to gather my thoughts; to start to look forward to my work. I am, again, in the place called Stansted House. I walk through the many halls and I see the faces of those who have come, with great expectations, to be taught and to be helped by those who have the knowledge to take them further on their path. I come with a specific reason in mind because I know that the one I will use will be there and I, at last, will be able to make contact with her. I am quite apprehensive as to whether things will be right for me to be able to place myself fully with her so that she will realise that it is truly I, and not someone who is coming who is pretending to be as I. I see in her face, too, an eagerness, for the very atmosphere of the place seems to fill her with joy. I see this joy with many who come. It is as though the very walls are filled with the essence of love and spiritual understanding.

I see the many classes and I listen; and in some ways, I am learning because I see the different methods of teaching, different thoughts on a theme, and I am pleased to think that, perhaps, in some way, I had a part in this.

Now, I am drawn towards the child and I am able to use her and I am pleased. I will not give details of my first contact with her but all that is necessary for me to say is that contact was made and I was able to express myself through her. I knew then that the possibility of what lay ahead could become a reality, and I was pleased.

Now, I am journeying again through life. I walk forward with my companion and I see light ahead. I ask, by thought, 'what extra light can this be? It seems as though there is a brilliance that is beyond my thought, that seems to come'.

He smiles and says to me, 'This is when extra love is needed upon the earth plane – when there are times of toil and strife. When brother seeks to harm brother, then more light is given, more energy is used and more help is forthcoming to those in need. Those who, through their mental capacity cannot help themselves. Those who, perhaps through ignorance and lack of education are anxious to fight one another for possessions and material considerations. The light that comes from the realms above pervades the atmosphere and helps to bring about a solution. Perhaps, in Man's eyes, it does not seem to be the right solution, but you must remember that there are many factors involved and that, sometimes, something that seems not to be the right thing at that moment of time suddenly takes shape and the character of the people who have taken over in these countries can change – not always for the good – but sometimes there comes one who finds light and is able to help the people and does not wish to become a dictator. It is these people that we wish to help – ones who would help themselves, not to the detriment of their fellow man, but help themselves to be able to be more understanding and loving.'

As I go towards this light, I see that we are going into, as you would say, 'another dimension'. It is almost as though a secret door has been opened that we are permitted to go through at this moment of time. I am fully aware that I am in the presence of those who work in the realms of light because I see, not the coluor of their clothes, but a radiance of form. It is very difficult for me to be able to distinguish whether they, themselves, are male or female because, to me, the light is so bright.

My companion understands my thoughts and says to me that as I, myself, progress and go towards light, they will become more distinguishable, that I will be albe to see the true significance of their work. I feel quite privileged to be here. I feel as though I am a child who has stolen into a garden, a beautiful garden, where I have not had permission to go. I see the love here and I feel it radiating, and it seems as though all that is being given is energy. It is as though one generates energy and the other picks up the flow and then regenerates it and, as it passes from one to the other, it builds and builds.

I see the colours that are around and I realise that these souls are working on the colour rays that are sent to earth to be used by those who are healers upon the earth plane. Those who use all the colours to be able to help Man, and it is beautiful. It is as though everything is in colour. Everything is changing and moving in colour, as though the very thoughts that we have and the very air that we breathe is colour all around us. It is a wonderful feeling! I feel so regenerated. It is as though my whole being is regenerated by the rays of light and colour that are here, and I feel as though I want to place my hands on someone in need so that they, too, can feel this rejuvenation and love that comes.

Then I begin to realise fully how those who are dedicated to healing must feel when they are used as channels. I begin to truly wish that, when I was on the earth plane, I too, could have become a healer. I realise fully how wonderful it must have been on the earth plane when Jesus, the Christed one, walked and healed. How wonderful to have been clairvoyant at that time, to have been able to see the rays of colour that he used. I, again, feel inadequate, as though I have wasted time. Time I thought I was using rightly, I could have been using to help others. I send a prayer for those who are gifted with healing, that they may find the love and this light; that they may be used to the fullness of their capacity.

Then my companion beckons and I move on. It is as though I am being privileged, this day, to see many things. You do not only see – you feel and you re-live this very energy. It is so much a part of everything that you, yourself, become a part of everything. It is very hard to describe, but it is as though you have been dematerialised and come again with a newness of life.

I begin to truly understand the workings of God and the love. I know this is a word I have used many times in this short synopsis of life here, and I know it is hard for you upon the earth plane who have to live everyday lives, sometimes without much thought of love, to understand what it is like to live in an atmosphere of pure love. It is the purity of thought that counts. You children of light (I say 'of light' because it is always sent towards you) must realise that you yourselves, are capable of giving love to othrs and that you must lead lives so that other people will benefit from knowing you. Just as the woman who touched the hem of Jesus' garment was healed, sometimes a little love given by you to your fellow man can heal a rift that has been in that person – a rift that has taken them away from their fellow man because of something that has happened to cause a blight upon their lives.

I say to you that God's love is as an endless chain. One link builds to form strength by joining with another, and so on, till this chain of love is formed. It is a band, a golden band of spiritual understanding. It is not a chain that you would feel was a burden upon you, but a chain that gives you strength and courage to be able to face up to situations, as I, in my own life, have had to face up to situations. It is very hard for us, in human life , to realise that there are some things that we will never be able to achieve. There are some loves we will never be able to fulfill and, sometimes, it is the thought of unrequited love which is the most terrible burden to have to face, but I say to you, who think you are without love, that you must remember the love of God is always around you. You are not forgotten in any way and, even when you think that everything around is finished, there is new light and love being directed towards you to give you the stength to take the next step in life. I, myself, am now beginning to understand that the true purpose of my work must be to bring love and understanding to all Mankind.

CHAPTER 16

My New Look at Life Ahead

Again, I am with the light and I see my way clear ahead. It is as though I am walking through the mists of time towards this great light, and I feel free in my heart because I am taking no burdens with me. I have crossed all my bridges and I am leaving nothing behind that I wish to hold with me, so now I feel free to go forward and explore further into this world.

I know that, as I go on my journey, there will be many changes of thought that I shall have and I know that, many times, I will look back, in contemplation, on what I have already assessed and stored in knowledge. I realise that, to those who have come to read what has been written for me, they will not always agree with my points of view, but this will not deter me from going forward and endeavouring to bring more truth towards those left upon the earth plane. I feel very privileged to be able to do this work; to be able to continue to be useful. It is very important, my friends, that, when you turn into spirit life, you make yourself useful to help your fellow man. Not only the ones who are in spirit life with you, but also those who remain – those who, in some ways are ignorant of the fact of the spirit world and the earthly existence; those who seem to be tied down by material conditions, who seem to be, as you would say, 'absorbed in their own lives' so much that they cannot look at anything else. They see nothing of the beauty of God's understanding and love. They cannot absorb the thought of life after death. I feel that it is my duty to be able to give happiness to those who, now, are in fear of the word 'death'.

There is no death, my friends – this, I have proven myself. There is no death, but there is a continued exstence of life which is more important than the earthly life in many ways, because it is a time when you are able to look truly and squarely at yourself. To be able to fully understand your lack of knowledge and your own selfishness; to be able to truly say, 'I was this person, but now I am changed – and that, my friends, is a very great statement of life because we, ourselves, do not like change or anything that comes, as you would say, 'to rock the boat' of life. We wish for everything to go smoothly so that we can indulge ourselves in many ways. But, in spirit life, there is no need for this indulgence. You are able to assess and learn, and then you are able to teach others, which is the most important factor of all – to be able to bring this knowledge to others.

This is my main purpose now in journeying upon this land – to be able to bring to others the knowledge I am gaining. To some it may seem as though it is trivial, but to others it will reach a part of their soul which will cause the light to burn brightly and a love and understanding to build up towards their fellow man. There will be some people who will be touched by my words, and there will be others who will not hear. Feel sorry for the ones who cannot listen or be taught anything because they have much to look forward to in the new life that is ahead of them, and much work to bring them to full understanding. Those who have open minds are halfway there. They are able to assimilate, able to assess themselves and able to accept God's will in many ways. I, myself, little realised the true meaning of God's will and the God-given will that I, myself, was empowered with when on the earth plane. How many of us have changed our destinies by our own pig-headedness? How many of us have decided that, no, we will not go with the tide of life, we will swim strongly against it?

Even though we make no headway, we will still, as you would say, 'knock our heads against the wall', we still continue to utilise self in so many ways. We will still continue to have our own selfish, egotistical frame of mind, and we will not look to the knowledge that others have tried to impart to us – others who have gone through these circumstances that I now find myself in which, to all intents and purposes, is called 'death'.

I am proud that I am able to come to help other people. This is the most important thing of all – love of one another; to love each other as ourselves; to think not of the cost of our own personal time; to be able to think of other people's feelings and follow through with help – not only the monetary help that can be given in many cases of need, but also to think of the giving of oneself, of one's time, of one's thought to others. There are many dear friends upon the earth plane who sit, day and night, sending out loving thoughts of healing towards people who are quite unaware of their care for them, and it is before souls such as these that I would wish for my work to be placed. Then they can see how their thoughts can be utilised to help Mankind.

How much the power of thought is a living thing and we, ourselves, are eternal life. No matter how many times we return to earth life, or how many times we walk in a different costume of life, we, ourselves, are truly spirit and it is only by the light being shed from the God-head that we manifest ourselves in a true manner. When you look at some people, you can see that their auric field is not clear, and that the problems of life are weighing them down. When you see this with a friend, send thought towards them to help them, to give them a new perspective of life, so they realise that there is something greater beyond our ken. Man is nothing and God is all; help them to accept that we are insignificant in His universe and His thoughts – that we, ourselves, are just a small part of a chain of events and that we must make the most of our knowledge and forethought to be able to generate the true love of God upon the earth plane. We should not bore people with our own thoughts as regards religion, telling them how we are pious and go to church regularly. We must not take on an attitude of 'holier than thou' – it is not that, my friend, that is the true lesson of life. It is being able to accept that you, yourself, can be inferior. That you will always find someone else who is greater and more acceptable than yourself. You must understand that this is a case of trying very hard to be true to yourself and true to your Father, God, for He knows all that is around you; nothing is hidden. There is no act upon this earth that is not registered. You may think that, if no-one sees what you are doing, then you have escaped without being called to answer for these actions, but I say to you, my friends, that everything you think and do upon the earth plane is registered and, when you realise that this is so, you will be in full understanding of how important it is how you lead your life.

People may say: it is impossible for everything to be monitored; but I say to you that there are more things in Heaven and Earth than we can ever understand. Yet, when understanding comes, things are more simple than you would ever think possible. So I say to you, my friends, that, if you are willing to listen awhile, then I will endeavour, through my lifetime in spirit, to bring forth more truth towards you. But, as I say, it is your choice as to whether you will stay awhile with me.

CHAPTER 17

Out of the Blue

How many times, in childhood, have we been told that Heaven is above us, in the sky, in that clear, blue void? And how many times has this misconception been placed in the minds of innocent children – that they go to live in a world that is far away? Yet, my friends, my world is entwined with yours. I can be close to you and I can be far away; and it is with this knowledge that those who have lost loved ones will begin to understand and realise that, with the power of love and thought, they can be constantly near, helping and loving even more so than when they were in earthly life, because they are not bound by the earthly environments. They are able to truly be themselves. The spiritual you comes forward and the light that is within your soul comes forward also to shine through you.

I say to you who have lost parents and children, not to worry, because I have seen many happy groups since I have been here. I see the children playing happily and content, just as though they are in nursery school or boarding school. They are happy and content and they forget the passage of time. They are nurtured and loved by those in spirit who are drawn to them. They are never left to worry or to fret.

Then I see the older people who have passed into spirit who have been so weary, so tired of earthly exhistence. Those to whom the journey into life has, perhaps, been a very great and vast experience of bitterness and pain so it seems to them as though there is nothing in life for them, until they come to the realisation that the many lessons they have learnt in that life have given them more openness to spiritual life. They are more able to assimilate the knowledge of the love of God. They are truly great in stature. It is not the ones who have a lazy time upon the earth plane who gain when they come into spirit; it is those who have led exemplory lives, those who have been, perhaps, hard-working, of working-class families; those who have had little or nothing in life that they could say was their own. Thus, when it came time for them to pass into spirit, they had no worry or care about things that they would leave behind, because they knew that all they would be leaving was a loving memory in someone's mind. Someone would remember them with love and understanding and, to them, that was more important than anything else.

I say to you: never worry over the animals that come into spirit life, for they play, they are happy and content, and they join with ones whom they had joined with on the earth plane (members of families). They are quite content to wait until the one who was their master upon the earth plane passes into spirit so they can be reunited, and until the time comes for them to go into the big sleep so they can go back into the source of all life to be replenished and re-formed to come in another way. But of that I will talk much later, because it is a most important factor of spirit life and progression. We all have to start from somewhere. As it has been thought upon the earth plane, that people started from one-celled creatures and grew into other species with the evolution of life, so the animals have their part to play. Even the plants and the trees have their part to play and we, as human beings, have our part to play also – to look after the animals and the vegetation and not to pollute the atmosphere; to be able to hand on to the next generation this beautiful world that God provided for us. This beautiful earth that grows with profusion the food that is needed, with the sunlight that comes to warm the day, and the moon that comes to guide those that have to travel by night. So, you see, we must remember that this is our heritage to look after during the time that we are on the earth plane – this wonderful creation – so that Man can go on in his search for knowledge; so that Man can return again to partake of a way of life; to be able to, as he progresses, find true understanding. There are many things that I would like to say at this moment of time, but I feel that I must take you gently forward because Man is not able to assess unless it is, as you would say, 'spoonfed' to him. He is not able to fully accept and to understand immediately. He must think and think again, and then think again, because it is the last thought that is important. It is that last thought, when you leave behind your earthly existence, not to fight and struggle to remain upon the earth, but to hold yourself in readiness for the rebirth into spirit life. To look forward to it, not as a curse, but as a blessing. A new beginning, a new understanding, a new drawing nearer to God's love, a new looking at oneself and a new loving for the ones you leave behind, because there is no animosity here, there is no bad feeling, So you, my friends, on the earth plane, who have, as you would say, been 'saddled' with someone who has been a very difficult partner in life or a difficult member of the family, do not fear, when you return to spirit life, because this will not exist. The animosity and bad feeling will not exist any more. It is as though a great light has come and washed away all feeling of ill, all feeling of mis-content, and only a feeling of true understanding and light and love remains, so you will not be drawn, again, towards this animosity that has been with you and the person in question. You will find that this has been completely erased, as though some great hand has been placed upon you – someone who, with loving care, lifts away all thought, all trouble and tribula-tion – that renews and regenerates. And you, in your heart, will rejoice because you will be then in full understanding of the light that is shed by God.

There is no worry over earthly things and, as regards

Heavenly things, you will find that there is very much similarity between this world and your world. There is always this light , this wonderful light, and there are always those who will come from other realms to help. There are always those who will give their light to help you, to make you understand the love that is within you, the love that is there to be given to others, because no-one upon the earth plane realises the full potential of love. We think of things in a more physical manner. We do not realise that it is pure, spiritual love that is the most important thing of all. Those with whom we have been spiritually attuned; those with whom we have felt on a level; those with whom we have felt as brothers; this is the most important feeling of all. I say to you that, when you return to spirit life, it is as if, out of the blue, full understanding comes, with the knowledge that is important for your journey in this life.

CHAPTER 18

A Settlement of Thought

Each time I become conscious of my surroundings, I wonder. I realise the thought that must have gone into the making of this wonderful place; how each thought is taken and used, and how each of us, in turn, must have thought for each other before this place can become manifest in the manner in which I now see it, with the beauty and light that is here and the complete understanding of God's force.

I look back upon my life on the earth and the many thoughts that circulated in my mind. How foolish I must have been in many ways! I remember the quite foolish thoughts I had in my youth, and then, again, when I reached my middle years of life. I look again at the thought pattern, and I realise that, even then, when I surmised that I was fully aware of everything that I should be aware of, I was not, and I begin to realise how much I must learn in this place and how much you, my friends, must also assimilate and accept when you come on the journey that I have taken.

My purpose in coming to you is to help to send a light forward so that, when you come, you will know there is someone who cares about your journey and the way that you will come. Someone who has thought towards you to help you bring yourself forward with an openness of mind. Many people close themselves up completely in life, and they become as an oyster in the seabed. They only seem to open themselves towards their close family or towards those who would attend to them and would be as body servants to them. Yet, by keeping themselves in such a cloistered and closed atmosphere, they do not realise what they are losing. You must never be afraid to face life. You must never take a cowardly action to absolve you from life. You must face it squarely and truly within yourself and you must be true to yourself and true to all that you hold dear and your principles about life. Unless you can truly face up to thought, then, my friends, you have come on a wasted journey on the earth plane and you will never fully understand the reason for your being there.

In how you treat each other, is the way you progress. It is how your thought and mind work towards helping others, that determines how you progress, and it is only when you send bad thought and bad actions towards others that you digress. If you keep this simple thought in mind, you will find that you will be able to go forward with much joy and under-standing, and that your life will take on more meaning. Your tread, your step, will be much lighter and you will be able to face everything that comes your way with a joy inside. The challenge you will see as another test along life's way, another trial to be faced – something that you, alone, can overcome. As you go on and progress in this manner, you will see that there is nothing in God's Heaven that you could not face and there is nothing in life upon the earth that you also could not face.

So many people are afraid of the word 'death'. They build up so many taboos about certain words in society. At one time, there was an issue of bodily behaviour that became a word that must not be used. Now, this word is bandied about, and a simple word like 'death' is thought to be a terrible thing to discuss – something that we do not wish to hear of until it is necessary for us to talk about it. Yet I say to you that it is no harder a stage to go through than the birth. It is no less a pattern of life than anything else. It is just the door that opens to take you into your new life – to your new surroundings. It is something that comes with a gentle hand to lead you, to take you forward.

You see, thought is everything. You can do nothing without thought. Your brain cannot activate your body without thought. If thought was not sent to your little finger to move, then it would not move. And so it is with everything in life. It is what you put into your life with thought that counts. If you are one who uses negative thought, nothing you try to achieve will ever come to pass; and if you are one who bulldozes through life with too positive a thought, then you will find that friends will drop from you and people will never understand you. But, if you take a balance of the negative and the positive, you become a more well-balanced person, and people draw close to you because they know that you are a person of common-sense. You are someone with whom they can discuss a point because the thought that you would put forward would not be biased or of your own opinion, but would be a thought that would be able to generate knowledge and understanding and, my friends, in life, there are many of us who need understanding. There are many frustrated people upon the earth plane who see nothing in life but the frustrations that lie ahead. They do not realise that, when they go into sleep-state, they are immediately helped by the ones who draw close to them. The answers are given to them, if only they will let the small, still voice of conscience speak to them. If only that small, still voice that comes from God, the Father, is allowed to be heard, then they will find the true answer to all their problems and the misunderstandings of life. There are many people who, by little things, have had their lives spoiled, and blighted. There are those who have read into another person's actions more than was there. There are others who have read too little into another person's actions and so someone who has deeply loved has been turned aside.

You see, there is so much that is controlled by thought. I

leave you with this thought, to make your own way and your own progress, but to remember my words – that thought is the mother of all things.

CHAPTER 19

My Progress, and my Love Towards Fellow Man

Yes, I am making progress. I realise this because my heart becomes much lighter within me, and I am able to accept, more readily, things that come towards me to teach me. I begin to realise that, in the world I am now in, there is so much to be learnt, so much to find; and I have brought you just a little way along the road that I am travelling.

My friends, it will not be a wasted journey because, at this moment of time, I must withdraw and go forward, to make my progression. In my journeying forward, I will again come and bring more knowledge and truth towards you. I have as yet only given you a glimpse into this new life because it is important that you should take the knowledge in easy steps. Then you, yourselves, can assimilate and understand fully the true significance of after-life.

There are so many things that I, myself, will have to learn and I ask you to bear with me as I go forward in my stage of evolution. I hope I will be able to take you with me on my journey to show you the new force and understanding that I will meet and the new ones who come from the realms of spirit to be near the people of earth to help them. The ones who have many different ways of their life to lead; the ones who draw close to those who are in darkness to help them; the ones who come to earth to be with mediums and sensitives, to be teachers and to be guides.

There is so much work here, and so much love for you, my friends. You will never be able to understand the true meaning of God's will and His love. It is only as you progress in spirit to such a level that you are drawn into light that you will truly understand His love and the full meaning of the work that is done here. I have only touched lightly on different subjects because I have felt that it would be unwise to bring too much knowledge, too quickly, because we are all on different levels of thought and it is impossible for all of us to be on the same level at the same time. So there will be many of you, unfortunately, who will not be fully able to assimilate and understand the knowledge which will come. But, to the ones who find that they can read my words with an open mind and a thirst for knowledge, then, my friends, my endeavour will be to take you further along on the journey with me.

I feel regret, at this moment of time, that I must withdraw, but you must understand that the ones who are used have their own lives upon the earth plane to live, and we, in spirit, are only too grateful for the time and the love that they give towards us so that we may manifest. I say to you, be thoughtful to those who are sensitive because their lives are most difficult. They have to have difficulty in life so that they can have true understanding of all facets of life, so that they can help others who are in need. Unless they, themselves, have experienced sorrow and loss of love, and pain, they, in their turn, cannot be sympathetic. So you see, my friends, again, thought comes – thought for others – it is important and it is a thing that we think of too lightly and put aside from ourselves.

So I leave you now, and I say: May God's blessing be with you until I come again.